DRAKE TANDRIST

Take Me To Naboo

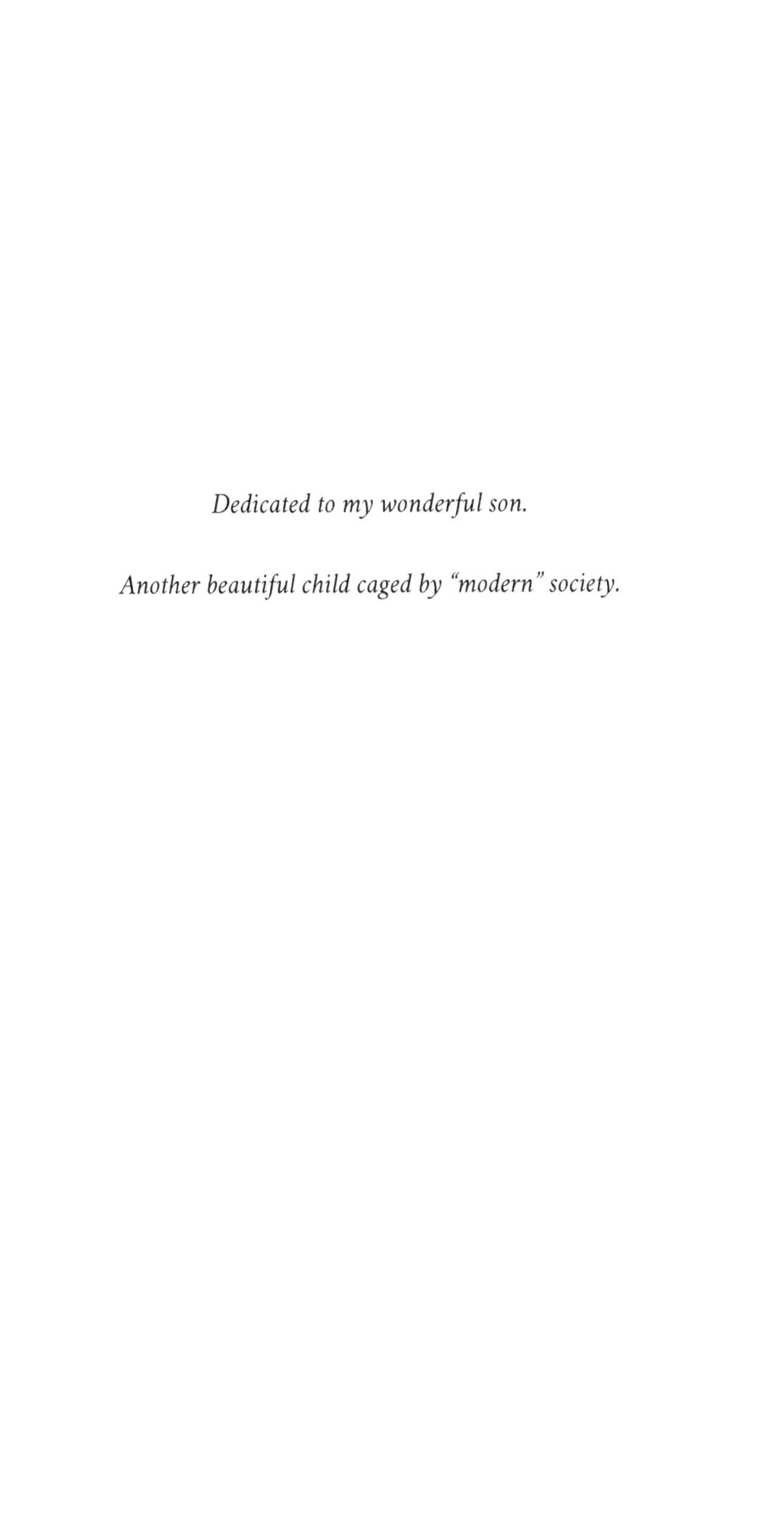

Dedicated to my wonderful son.

Another beautiful child caged by "modern" society.

Contents

Introduction

September 22, 2024. The world is embroiled in numerous conflicts, each with its own history, drivers, and human cost. According to the Council on Foreign Relations' Global Conflict Tracker, there are currently over 25 significant ongoing crises worldwide, affecting regions from the Americas to Sub-Saharan Africa.

Each of these conflicts varies in scale, but their impact is universally felt—by families torn apart, by displaced populations, and by nations struggling to find stability amidst chaos. Let's pause and think about what this means.

Right now, countless people are affected by war, violence, and instability. According to the list of ongoing armed conflicts on Wikipedia, which draws data from the Armed Conflict Location & Event Data Project (ACLED), there have already been at least 147,547 fatalities in 2024. In 2023, the number of recorded deaths reached 158,477. These casualties however represent only a fraction of the total human toll in war. For each life lost, there are many more who are wounded— physically, mentally, or both. According to ACLED's Conflict Index, 1 in 7 people are estimated to have been exposed to conflict so far in 2024, and 50 countries rank in their index categories for extreme, high, or turbulent levels of conflict.

How many of these victims are civilians—people who had no part in the decisions that led to war, yet found themselves entangled in its horrors? In modern conflict, the lines between combatants and civilians are blurred. Bombings, airstrikes, and raids often take place in residential areas, turning homes, schools, and hospitals into battlegrounds. Does it sound as a surprise that, sometimes, as many as 90% of casualties are civilians—innocent people forced to flee, to fight for survival, or to grieve those they've lost?

And yet, what drives these conflicts? How many wars are waged not for survival or defense, but for greed—for power, for resources, for money? History is littered with examples of conflicts fueled by the desire for control over land, oil, minerals, or strategic advantage. Many wars have complex roots, but economic and geopolitical interests often underpin the violence. From multinational corporations that profit from war economies to nations vying for dominance, many conflicts have layers of hidden agendas.

As a political theorist, Thomas Hobbes once suggested that greed and hunger for power are intrinsic parts of the human condition—but is this truly so? Are we really in a war of all against all? Is this the natural state humankind would be in without the "protection" of a sovereign authority? What if it weren't? Many have imagined a world where greed no longer dictated the course of human history. A world where disputes could be settled through dialogue, where resources were shared, and where power was redefined not by control but by cooperation. Imagine all the people living a life in peace. Imagine even there are no countries. It isn't hard to do, but it takes a lot of courage to step away from the forces that have shaped our world for so long—to reject the systems of division, power, and greed that have driven us into conflict, and to build a new paradigm where cooperation, compassion, and mutual respect are the foundations of a shared human future.

This book is about that journey—toward a new paradigm for humanity, one that challenges and perhaps surpasses many outdated views that have governed our world for centuries. While democracy, as it exists today, has often been hailed as the pinnacle of human governance, we must ask ourselves: does the current version of democracy truly reflect the ideals it claims to uphold? Or has it, in some places, become a relic of systems designed in an era long gone—systems that now struggle to address the complexities of our interconnected, globalized world?

Democracy, in its purest form, promises participation, representation, and the protection of individual rights. Yet, in many cases, it has been distorted by entrenched power structures, corruption, and the manipulation of public opinion. The result? A system that too often serves the few, rather than the many. This isn't to say that democracy should be discarded, but instead that it must evolve. Some aspects of our traditional political and economic systems—bureaucracies that hinder progress, outdated laws that fail to address modern challenges, and power structures that benefit from division—belong in a museum, so to speak. It's time to re-imagine governance for the future, perhaps by incorporating the very tools that define our age.

Advances in science and technology offer us the chance to create systems of governance that are more transparent, more accountable, and more in tune with the needs of people. What if we could leverage artificial intelligence and blockchain technology to ensure fairness in elections, transparency in decision-making, and the equitable distribution of resources? What if technology could facilitate direct, real-time participation in governance, empowering individuals and communities to shape their own futures? These possibilities are not far-fetched—they are within reach, if we have the courage to question the status quo and embrace innovation.

This book will explore how we might move beyond traditional systems of governance, economy, and society to create new alternatives that are better suited to a world defined by complexity and rapid change. It is a journey of human evolution—one that asks us to rethink how we live, work, and coexist on this planet. As we move forward, we must remain mindful of the lessons of the past, but unafraid to chart a new course for the future.

To make this book more practical and engaging, it will go beyond theoretical concepts and offer something actionable—steps that can be taken to apply the ideas in daily life or to explore new ways of thinking. Each chapter will feature a "to do", designed not only for reflection but also to encourage active involvement, self-challenge, and the pursuit of new knowledge and experiences. These action points will give readers the tools to take ownership of their learning journey and help them connect the ideas in this book to real-world contexts.

For example, after reading a chapter on rethinking governance, readers might be prompted to research local grassroots movements in their area, or even explore how technologies like blockchain are being used for transparent decision-making. It could be as simple as encouraging someone to have a conversation with someone from a different political background, to understand their perspective better, or as ambitious as challenging them to propose a small change in their community that could have a ripple effect on governance.

These "to dos" aren't just about self-reflection, but about stepping out of comfort zones—whether mentally or physically. They aim to bridge the gap between theory and practice, nudging readers to become agents of change themselves. Whether through personal development, community engagement, or learning about innovations in science and technology, these prompts will provide a pathway for readers to discover new perspectives, interact with others, and start making changes on an individual and collective level.

No matter how challenging the world around us may seem, there is always room for inspiration. Even in times when courage feels distant and the weight of indifference, greed, and intolerance threatens to overshadow hope, we remain resilient—by nature or by necessity. Humanity has a deep-rooted ability to persevere, to find strength in adversity, and to seek beauty where it still thrives.

The world, after all, is far too extraordinary, too vibrant, to allow it to be further marred by forces that divide and destroy. Its oceans, forests, and mountains—its cultures, its people—deserve more than to be overshadowed by narrow ambitions. There is always hope, a spark that cannot be extinguished, to improve both ourselves and the world around us. This book is a reminder that despite everything, change is possible. It invites us not only to reflect but to act—to take a stand against indifference and embrace the courage to create a more compassionate, sustainable future.

The path to a better world starts with the courage to imagine it.

I

The Basics

1

Equality

Every single person on earth is equal.

Most of us have probably made the mistake of thinking we're somehow better than others, whether it's due to social status, cultural background, or life experiences. But where does this belief come from? Is it deeply ingrained in human nature, or is it something learned? At its core, we are all born into this world with the same fundamental needs, vulnerabilities, and capacity for growth. Yet, the idea that we differ in worth is a construct that keeps evolving over time. Evolutionarily, humans have developed hierarchies for survival and societal structure, but the truth is, these hierarchies are arbitrary when it comes to human value. Strip away the cultural, political, and economic layers, and we are all connected by a shared humanity.

At the most basic level, every human being is born with the same needs for survival, belonging, love, and dignity. These commonalities form the foundation of our shared existence, reminding us that beyond the systems and structures that often divide us, we all experience the same human condition. We all have the same capacity for empathy, vulnerability, and resilience. We experience emotions like joy, grief, and fear in much the same way, regardless of nationality or status. This shared humanity means that no one person's life is inherently more valuable than another's. We all deserve the same respect and rights, not because of where we come from or what we have, but simply because we exist as human beings. Recognizing this can help us foster greater understanding and compassion, reminding us that we are more alike than we are different.

Think about respect—don't we all crave it? To be recognized, treated with dignity, and seen as valuable individuals? Yet, how often do we fail to extend the same courtesy to others? Perhaps it's because we've been conditioned to compete, or because we find it hard to understand perspectives different from our own. But in reality, it's remarkably simple to show respect. It's not about agreeing with everyone's beliefs or choices, but about acknowledging their right to exist and pursue their own path. Respect for someone's being, convictions, aspirations, and dreams can be a powerful gesture. It shows that despite our differences, we recognize the shared desire for meaning and dignity in life. What would it take to make respect the baseline for how we treat others? A simple pause, a moment to remember that everyone carries their own struggles, dreams, and stories.

The fight for equality is a longstanding struggle that has profoundly influenced the course of human history. From ancient revolts against oppressive rulers to modern-day movements, this pursuit has shaped civilizations by challenging systems of power and privilege. Every time though, they reflect humanity's inherent desire for fairness and justice, rooted in the belief that all people should be treated with equal dignity. They demonstrate that the journey toward equality is deeply embedded in our collective consciousness, often motivated by the basic principle that no individual should be treated as lesser than another. However, this fight is still ongoing because entrenched systems of inequality don't easily give way. Power structures have historically resisted changes that threaten privilege and hierarchy.

When we discuss equality, the distinction between equality of opportunity and equality of outcome is central to understanding how fairness is approached in society.

Equality of opportunity focuses on leveling the playing field. It's the idea that everyone, regardless of their background, should have access to the same resources and opportunities—such as education, healthcare, and employment. The aim is to provide the necessary tools and environments that allow individuals to thrive based on their abilities, efforts, and choices. This concept values fairness and meritocracy, where the role of society is to remove barriers such as discrimination, poverty, or lack of access that prevent people from realizing their potential.

Equality of outcome takes a different approach. It recognizes that, even with equal opportunities, not everyone will achieve the same level of success. Equality of outcome suggests that, for true fairness, there should be mechanisms to ensure that resources and success are more evenly distributed among all members of society, regardless of their starting point or circumstances. This might involve redistributive policies like wealth taxes or social safety nets, aiming to reduce disparities in income, health, and well-being.

The tension between these two forms of equality is significant. One could argue that emphasizing opportunity alone is insufficient because historical and social factors continue to shape people's outcomes.

For example, even with access to the same schools, children from wealthier families may have other advantages—like tutoring, stable home environments, or professional networks—that set them ahead. On the other hand, focusing solely on outcome equality can be seen as limiting personal freedom and incentive, as individuals might feel less motivated to excel if they know their results will be redistributed.

Exploring this balance offers a more nuanced view of equality in practice. It invites a conversation about the ethical implications of how society allocates resources and whether equality means everyone starting in the same place or ending in similar circumstances. Contemporary debates, such as those around affirmative action, universal basic income, and tax reform, revolve around this distinction—showing that the challenge is not just creating opportunities, but ensuring that the outcomes they lead to are just and equitable.

Zooming in on equality of opportunity, it is both a moral imperative and a collective necessity in a world teeming with diverse talents, perspectives, and potentials, to advocate for and ensure opportunities for every individual on this planet. It's a plea that embodies a vision for a global society where every person, regardless of their birthplace or nationality, is afforded equal chances to pursue their dreams, contribute to society, and lead fulfilling lives. Such a world is not only more just but infinitely richer in innovation, creativity, and progress.

Freedom of opportunity is the cornerstone of a fair and equitable world. It means that every child, no matter where they are born, has access to quality education that nurtures their talents and interests. It means that every young adult can choose their path without barriers imposed by their geography, socio-economic status, or the political climate of their homeland. It means that every person can aspire to better living conditions, healthcare, and the chance to participate in a global economy on equal footing.

Yet, the reality we face is starkly different. The lottery of birth determines not just life's starting point but often its trajectory and destination. Consider this a reflection of our collective failure to dismantle the barriers we have erected—barriers that confine talent, ambition, and hope within man-made borders. This oversight carries a substantial cost for society, as it dims the light on some of the potential for groundbreaking discoveries, transformative innovations, and valuable contributions that could emerge, were they not stifled by the grip of inequality.

This plea for freedom of opportunity is also a call to action. It urges nations, corporations, and individuals to recognize the inherent value in every person and to work tirelessly to create a world where opportunities are not hoarded but shared. It calls for the dismantling of the physical and bureaucratic barriers that restrict movement and access to opportunities. It demands an investment in global education, healthcare, and infrastructure to level the playing field. It advocates for policies that foster collaboration over competition, solidarity over isolationism, and empathy over apathy.

Imagine a world where every person can truly thrive, where the innovations and cultural contributions of all peoples are celebrated and utilized for the betterment of humanity, and where cooperation transcends geographical divides, fostering solutions to global challenges like climate change, poverty, and disease. This is not a utopian fantasy but a feasible reality, if we commit to making freedom of opportunity a universal right, not a privileged exception.

The path towards this vision is obviously challenging, fraught with complexities and resistance from entrenched interests. Yet, the journey is as noble as its destination is worthy. By pledging to ensure freedom of opportunity for all, we sow the seeds for a more prosperous, equitable, and harmonious world.

What can you do? On a personal level, you can foster empathy for others' circumstances and become aware of one's own privileges. By recognizing the challenges others face, people can take small steps—such as mentoring someone from an underprivileged background, donating to educational causes, or volunteering time for social justice initiatives—that make a difference in creating equal opportunities. On a broader scale, individuals can engage in political processes that support equality, or in community efforts that promote equal access to resources—such as water, food, shelter, education, healthcare and other basic human rights.

If you truly want to make a difference, pay it forward.

It's a simple yet profound philosophy: changing someone's life in a positive way without them asking for it, simply because you can. When you give without expectation, you're not just performing a good deed, you're creating a ripple effect—a change that could alter the trajectory of someone's life for the better. Whether it's opening a door for a person who didn't even know they had one, offering guidance, or creating an opportunity, your actions can be the catalyst that propels them forward. And often, the greatest impacts are made when you expect nothing in return, remaining unseen and allowing the spotlight to fall on the person you've helped.

Think about the moments in your own life when someone extended a helping hand—whether big or small. Maybe they believed in you when others didn't, or they created a space for you to grow in ways you hadn't imagined. These acts of kindness, these doors opened unexpectedly, are what many of us remember as pivotal points in our personal journeys. Now, imagine being that person for someone else. It's not about grand gestures or recognition, but rather the quiet, impactful actions that lead to real change.

Paying it forward goes beyond charity. It's about empowerment. It's about giving someone the tools, knowledge, or opportunity to change their life in a way they may never have thought possible. Maybe it's recommending them for a job they're perfect for, mentoring someone who just needs the right advice, or funding an education without the recipient even knowing where the money came from. The possibilities are endless, and the rewards—although not seen immediately—are profound.

This call to action is more than just a suggestion; it's an invitation to be a force for good in the world. Make a difference, not for applause or recognition, but because you can. Because in paying it forward, you're helping to create a world where kindness, opportunity, and hope can thrive. The impact you leave behind may not be celebrated, but it will be felt, and it will inspire others to do the same. This is how we build a better future—one quiet, powerful gesture at a time.

2

Borders

We do not need borders. No, we don't.

Historically, borders have emerged from a complex interplay of geography, culture, politics, and power. They were not always the rigid lines we recognize today but evolved from more fluid concepts tied to natural features like rivers, mountains, and forests. Early human settlements were often defined by such natural landmarks, which served as boundaries separating tribes or communities. As societies grew more organized, political entities like city-states, kingdoms, and empires began to form. These early societies often expanded through conquest or alliances, and their borders were typically drawn in response to military power, resource control, and strategic considerations.

The first significant territorial borders can be traced back to ancient civilizations like Mesopotamia, Egypt, and China. For example, the Great Wall of China stands as one of history's most monumental border projects, designed to protect against invasions. In medieval Europe, the rise of feudalism also led to the establishment of boundaries, largely controlled by lords and monarchs, with territories often shifting due to wars, marriages, or treaties.

The concept of modern national borders, however, began to crystallize with the Peace of Westphalia in 1648, which marked the end of the Thirty Years' War in Europe. This treaty is considered a foundational moment in international law, introducing the idea of sovereign states with clearly defined borders that should not be violated by external powers. This Westphalian system laid the groundwork for the nation-state concept, where a government's authority is confined to a specific territory, and those within the borders share a national identity or allegiance.

Colonialism played a significant role in further defining global borders. As European powers expanded across the world, they arbitrarily divided vast continents such as Africa, Asia, and the Americas, often without regard for existing ethnic, cultural, or geographic divisions. These colonial borders, drawn primarily to serve imperial interests, have had long-lasting effects, contributing to numerous conflicts and divisions that persist to this day.

In the modern era, borders have continued to evolve, often shaped by the outcomes of wars, treaties, and decolonization. However, while borders are now often seen as fixed and inviolable, they remain deeply contentious. They are products of human history—of power struggles, cultural negotiations, and economic interests—rather than natural or inevitable divisions. Understanding their origins reminds us that borders are not immutable, and their purpose and justification can be questioned, especially when they cause more harm than unity.

Throughout history, the principle of nationality has often been used to justify the separation of peoples, leading to fragmentation rather than unity. National borders, drawn along ethnic, religious, or cultural lines, have repeatedly served as tools for division rather than for peace. Many times, these borders have been imposed by external forces or elites, without regard for the existing social or cultural ties among the people they separated.

What's troubling is that, even today, many leaders continue to promote the idea that borders are a key to peacekeeping and stability. They cling to the notion that the separation of peoples, based on nationality, ethnicity, or religion, is the best way to maintain order. Instead of addressing the underlying social and economic factors that often lead to conflict, they focus on reinforcing borders and isolating communities. Leaders in various parts of the world continue to advocate for national sovereignty and strict border control as solutions to complex global challenges, from migration to security, despite evidence that this often intensifies tensions and fosters division.

In today's interconnected world, this reliance on borders as a solution feels increasingly outdated. The world faces transnational issues like climate change, economic inequality, and mass migration—challenges that require cooperation rather than division. Despite this, many policymakers remain fixated on borders, failing to recognize that global collaboration, not separation, is the path to lasting peace. Leaders who promote walls, exclusionary policies, and rigid borders fail to address the root causes of conflict and inequality, perpetuating a cycle of division that undermines global stability. Their insistence on this approach reveals a troubling inability to learn from history's lessons, as the continued reliance on border-based solutions ignores the complexities of the modern world.

The concept of country borders represents not merely a geographical boundary but an invisible, yet potent, force that categorizes, segregates, and, most significantly, discriminates against individuals based solely on their place of birth. This form of discrimination, rooted in the arbitrary lines drawn on maps, dictates not just where individuals can live, work, and travel, but profoundly impacts their opportunities, rights, and freedoms. It is a discrimination so pervasive and deeply ingrained in the global socio-political fabric that it often goes unnoticed, yet its effects are monumental, making it arguably the highest form of discrimination faced by humanity.

From the moment of birth, an individual is ascribed a nationality—an arbitrary assignment that significantly influences their life trajectory. This categorization predetermines their access to healthcare, education, economic opportunities, and even the likelihood of experiencing conflict or peace. The disparities between nations, in terms of wealth, stability, and opportunity, mean that this form of discrimination is not just about social exclusion or prejudice but about life-and-death consequences.

Consider the refugee forced to flee their home due to war or persecution, only to find that borders are closed to them, their humanity disregarded in favor of political or economic considerations. Or the talented student, born in a developing country, whose potential contributions to science, art, or technology are stifled because educational and employment opportunities are gatekept behind the visa requirements of wealthier nations. These are not isolated incidents, but systemic manifestations of discrimination based on nationality.

Moreover, the enforcement of these borders often involves practices that violate basic human rights—from the separation of families to the detention of asylum seekers in conditions that strip them of dignity and hope. Such enforcement perpetuates a cycle of inequality and suffering that contrasts sharply with the ideals of freedom, equality, and justice that many nations purport to uphold.

In an increasingly interconnected world, where ideas, culture, and commerce flow freely across digital platforms, the insistence on maintaining rigid physical borders feels paradoxically outdated and counterproductive. It is a testament to a world order that prioritizes the sovereignty of states over the well-being of the global human community.

The highest form of discrimination, therefore, lies not in the overt acts of prejudice or hatred between individuals, but in the systemic, institutionalized discrimination embedded in the very concept of nation-states and their borders. It splits humanity not by individual qualities, virtues, or deeds, but by the random chance of one's birthplace—a factor entirely beyond an individual's control.

Addressing this profound injustice requires a reimagining of global governance, one that emphasizes human unity and equity over arbitrary divisions. It demands global solidarity and a commitment to policies that prioritize human rights, mobility, and equality above nationalistic interests. The challenge is formidable, but the pursuit of a world where every individual's worth and rights are not dictated by their birthplace is a noble and necessary endeavor for the future of humanity.

Remember that the borders that surround us, both physical and psychological, are not immovable. They have been imposed, often for reasons that serve the few rather than the many, and they are there to maintain control rather than foster connection. But borders don't have to limit you. Instead of accepting these artificial lines, seek out ways to push beyond them. It might not be easy, but it's a challenge worth taking on.

Ask yourself: where in your life do borders hold you back? Maybe it's the literal borders of nations, restricting your freedom to explore, work, or live in certain places. Or perhaps the borders are more figurative—social expectations, rules, or mental barriers that keep you confined. Start by questioning why these limitations exist in the first place. Who benefits from you staying within these boundaries? Why should others dictate where you can go and what you can achieve? The moment you start challenging these questions, you begin to dismantle the walls that have been built around you.

When you begin to challenge borders, you'll inevitably face resistance, often from those closest to you. Friends, family, and colleagues may not understand your motivations or desire to step outside the accepted norms. They may doubt your intentions or question your decisions, often because these challenges threaten their own comfort zones. Some may even ridicule or dismiss your actions as unrealistic or rebellious, clinging to the belief that these boundaries are necessary or immutable. But remember, this resistance is more a reflection of their fears and limitations than of your own.

As you continue to push past the limitations imposed by borders, it's crucial to recognize that many people live comfortably within them—sometimes even happily. They may believe that the life they're living, despite its restrictions, is not so bad after all. This sense of contentment often stems from the belief that their government or societal structure provides security and stability, fostering a golden cage mentality. It's an existence where they feel safe, perhaps even privileged, compared to others who face harsher circumstances. It's understandable why they might think this way, and in many cases, their feelings are valid given the comforts they experience.

However, this can sometimes resemble the psychological phenomenon of the Stockholm Syndrome, where people develop affection or loyalty toward those who control or limit them. In such cases, it can feel more comfortable to accept these restrictions rather than challenge them. Similarly, some prefer the illusion of stability that systems provide, much like the characters in The Matrix who choose the comforting simulation over the harsh realities of the real world. It's important to recognize that while you may see these borders as barriers to freedom, others may not feel the same, and that's okay.

Respect their choices, just as you wish for them to respect yours. Don't judge or belittle someone else's perspective, even if you disagree with it. Everyone has their own journey, and just as you seek to break free from imposed limitations, others may find solace or purpose in the structures they inhabit. It's essential to allow space for these differences while continuing to walk your own path toward self-liberation.

Awakening to the realization that these borders are arbitrary doesn't happen overnight. For some, this awareness comes quickly, while for others, it might take years or even a lifetime. The key is to stay the course, even when others don't yet see the path you're on. Trust in your own journey and your vision of freedom, knowing that by defying these limitations, you are laying the groundwork not just for yourself but for others who may one day follow in your footsteps. Transformation is often met with skepticism before it is embraced, and in time, you may find that those who once doubted you will come to respect, or even admire, your courage.

Don't forget though that breaking free from borders doesn't mean being reckless. Respect for others and for yourself must always guide your actions. But don't let the fear of failure or the discomfort of swimming upstream stop you. Pushing your boundaries—whether it's crossing into a new country, changing careers, or redefining your identity—can be an exhilarating experience. You may hit walls that seem insurmountable, but cracks and loopholes always exist. If you look closely enough, you'll find them.

You may encounter resistance, frustration, or setbacks, but this struggle is part of the process. Every time you find a way around a border, you take a step towards greater freedom—freedom of movement, of thought, of opportunity. So, challenge the borders that confine you. Circumvent them, bend them, break them if necessary. The world beyond those borders is vast, and it's yours to explore.

3

Violence

Every form of violence is unacceptable.

Historically, violence has often been seen as a response to threat, whether real or perceived, rooted in the primal instinct for survival. This could include threats to physical safety, status, resources, or identity. But while survival instincts are part of our human nature, violence is not a predetermined outcome—it is a response shaped by both internal and external conditions.

On a psychological level, violence can stem from feelings of fear, frustration, or anger. When people feel cornered or powerless, they may resort to aggression as a way to reclaim control. This is often seen in situations of personal conflict or in the dynamics of abuse, where violence becomes a method for exerting dominance or control over another person. Emotional trauma and mental health issues can also contribute, as they may distort perception and reduce one's ability to handle conflicts non-violently.

Social factors play a huge role as well. Violence often arises in environments where individuals feel deprived, oppressed, or marginalized. When people are denied basic rights or opportunities, or when they feel excluded from the benefits of society, they may see violence as a means of achieving justice, equality, or recognition. Systemic violence, such as institutional racism or economic inequality, often fuels a cycle of violence in communities, as individuals react to the systemic harm with personal acts of aggression.

Culturally, violence is sometimes normalized or even glorified, whether through media, politics, or historical narratives. When societies valorize violent behaviors—whether in warfare, crime, or even competitive sports—it can create an environment where violence is seen as an acceptable, even heroic, response to conflict.

Additionally, environmental factors, such as poverty, social instability, and exposure to violence in the home or community, can further increase the likelihood of violent behavior. These conditions often breed stress and hopelessness, which can manifest in violent acts.

Ultimately, violence arises from a combination of these forces—biological instincts, psychological vulnerabilities, social conditioning, and environmental pressures. However, it's important to acknowledge that humans also have a capacity for empathy, cooperation, and peaceful resolution. The challenge lies in addressing the root causes of violence and promoting ways to manage conflict without resorting to harm.

But what does it mean if violence is used against you, when it becomes a violation of both your physical and emotional integrity? It's not just about the physical act—it's a tool that strips away your sense of control and security, aiming to instill fear, submission, or harm.

Regardless of the circumstances, violence is inherently destructive, not only causing immediate damage but also leaving lasting emotional and psychological scars. It fundamentally violates a person's dignity and autonomy, asserting power in a way that disregards mutual respect and the sanctity of life.

Experiencing violence often leaves one feeling powerless and dehumanized. This can lead to a profound sense of vulnerability, anger, or confusion, especially if the violence is unprovoked or systemic, but remember that the use of violence often reveals more about the perpetrator than the victim. It is a reflection of their fear, insecurity, or desire for control. Violence can stem from desperation, anger, or a warped sense of justice, but it never justifies itself. When someone resorts to violence, it signals an inability—or unwillingness—to resolve conflict through dialogue, understanding, or compromise. As a victim, it's crucial to recognize that the violence inflicted upon you is not a testament to your worth, but rather to the aggressor's failure to respect the value of human life and dignity.

In the face of violence, resisting the urge to retaliate with violence is one of the greatest challenges. The strength lies not in mirroring the aggression but in maintaining a sense of self and the belief that you can influence outcomes, seeking justice through means that transcend the cycle of harm.

However, some types of resistance could be justified.

The conventional definition of violence as actions meant to "hurt people or cause damage" can paint all harm in a negative light, but this doesn't capture the full complexity of resistance, especially when it involves targeting infrastructure or resources instead of human beings. While violence against people is always wrong, dismantling or sabotaging tools of oppression, like weapons or strategic assets, can be seen as a form of legitimate resistance rather than outright destruction. Actions like disrupting an aggressor's supply chain or disabling harmful technologies can, in some contexts, be seen as a necessary strategy to protect lives and end violence, as long as it doesn't hurt any people!

While actions that don't physically harm individuals may seem less problematic, economic harm can still have significant consequences for people's livelihoods, well-being, and long-term security. Therefore, to prevent unintended consequences, resistance strategies need to carefully choose targets to avoid collateral damage to civilians and local economies, and focus on disabling oppressive military or technological assets without disrupting civilian infrastructure. Obviously, before resorting to sabotage, diplomatic or economic pressure strategies, like sanctions or boycotts, need to be explored, which can weaken an aggressor's capabilities without harming civilians. In other words, while dismantling harmful systems might seem justified, the long-term economic effects must be carefully considered, as these can indirectly cause harm to the very people resistance efforts aim to protect.

In summary, we must never be the initiators of aggression, and when we do respond, it should always be in ways that safeguard human life, ensuring no harm comes to people in the process.

When we say no to violence, we obviously say no to war.

It also means that we need to reject the industries and entities that profit from conflict, most notably weapons manufacturers and the governments that support or enable them. The global arms trade is a significant industry, generating billions of dollars annually. It supplies weapons not just for so-called national defense but also for offensive actions, civil wars, and conflicts where civilians are often the primary victims. By choosing to oppose violence and war, we inherently challenge the legitimacy of this industry.

According to Statista, the United States and China are unsurprisingly two of the largest armament manufacturers globally, generating hundreds of billions of dollars in revenue through the production of weapons and military technology. This economic behemoth is driven by a select number of powerful corporations, such as Lockheed Martin, which rely heavily on government contracts to sustain their production. In terms of global weapons exports, the U.S. again leads, followed closely by Russia and France, which hold similar market shares, while China and Germany also compete closely in this highly profitable sector. Just think about this for a little while.

The reality is that these nations, through their arms industries, fuel conflicts across the world. Weapons manufactured by these companies do not remain confined to "national defense" but are exported to countries engaged in civil wars, regional conflicts, and geopolitical tensions. For example, U.S. arms exports often find their way to volatile regions in the Middle East, while Russian weapons are supplied to countries with long histories of internal strife. European nations like France and Germany, despite positioning themselves as global peace advocates, are also heavily involved in arms exports to nations involved in ongoing conflicts.

It's not a secret that weapons manufacturers, often backed by powerful governments, play a pivotal role in perpetuating violence by providing the tools of war. Their interests are financially aligned with conflict and instability, as increased warfare drives up demand for weapons and military technologies. Some of the largest arms-producing companies are based in countries that also have substantial political influence on the global stage, allowing them to set agendas that, at times, promote military solutions over diplomatic ones.

By rejecting these manufacturers, we are taking a stand against an industry that benefits from human suffering. However, the influence of these companies extends beyond mere production—they often lobby policymakers to maintain or expand defense budgets, shape foreign policies, and even influence decisions on whether to engage in or escalate conflicts. Saying no to violence means confronting this complex web of profit, power, and political influence.

Such a stance requires a broader societal shift towards transparency, accountability, and an emphasis on peaceful conflict resolution. It means advocating for the cessation of arms exports, reducing national and international dependence on the arms industry, and promoting alternatives such as peace-building initiatives and economic investments in conflict resolution.

In this way, rejecting war and violence is not just about an individual's choice to abstain from aggression but about addressing the systemic drivers that fuel global conflicts.

While many of the world's leading nations continue to maintain large, powerful military forces, some countries have taken a radically different approach. Costa Rica is a notable example. In 1949, Costa Rica abolished its standing army, becoming one of the first countries in the world to do so. Article 12 of its Constitution not only eliminates the possibility of a permanent army but also underscores the country's commitment to peace. Costa Rica retains the right to form a military for national defense in times of need, but any such force would always be under strict civilian control.

This decision has allowed Costa Rica to prioritize social development over military expenditure, channeling resources toward education, healthcare, and environmental protection. It stands as a powerful reminder that national security doesn't have to rely on militarization and that alternative, peaceful governance models exist—even though this approach remains the exception rather than the rule on the global stage. Costa Rica's stance contrasts sharply with the aggressive military posturing of larger nations, demonstrating a different path toward stability and peace.

If we truly want to dismantle the arms industry, we need to focus on hitting where it hurts the most: the flow of money and resources that sustain it. Shutting down the supply chain, blocking logistics, and disrupting the financial networks behind arms manufacturing are the most direct ways to halt production. These industries don't exist in isolation—they rely on a complex web of suppliers, financiers, and logistical networks that keep their operations running. Stopping weapons production requires a coordinated and powerful intervention to break this system.

This kind of mission will require the involvement of individuals and organizations with significant influence and resources. Financial backers, raw material suppliers, transport companies—all of these are vulnerable points in the chain. Identifying these choke points and applying pressure, either through divestment, public exposure, or operational disruptions can be key strategies.

Moreover, the power lies in those who have the financial means to create major interruptions. High-net-worth individuals or entities with significant financial influence could use their capital to divest from or block key suppliers of raw materials or technology that the arms industry depends on. Public pressure could be placed on critical logistics companies that transport arms or components, incentivizing them to step away from such contracts. This would require a massive, well-coordinated movement to disrupt the flow of resources to these manufacturers, cutting off the very lifeblood of production. Yet, it's important to remember that while this might sometimes seem like an insurmountable task, it is far from impossible.

A critical factor is that every system has vulnerabilities. No industry, no matter how powerful, is invincible if the right weak points are identified and exploited. The arms industry may seem untouchable, but its reliance on complex supply chains, financial backers, and political alliances makes it susceptible to disruption. Even small victories—like convincing a single logistics company to stop transporting arms components—can have a ripple effect, sparking broader changes across the industry. Therefore, the challenge isn't about whether it's possible, but about organizing the will, resources, and strategy to make it happen.

This kind of approach aims to target the heart of the industry and forces us to think about radical, yet lawful, economic warfare against the production of weapons.

To take meaningful steps against the arms industry, the first course of action is to understand it from within. Mapping out the industry's landscape—its manufacturers, supply chains, and logistics—allows us to better comprehend how it operates and where its weak points lie. By revealing the flow of resources, from raw materials to the final distribution of weapons, you can begin to identify the crucial connections that sustain this industry.

Once you know how the system works, share what you have learned, so we're all better informed and equipped to explore ways to disrupt it, be it through advocacy, policy pressure, or drawing attention to specific actors involved in maintaining the flow of arms. By pooling insights and efforts, we're building a network of people committed to the same cause, amplifying the impact of our actions. The more people who understand the mechanisms behind the arms industry, the more effective the movement becomes. A shared mission, built on the foundation of shared knowledge, is the key to tackling an issue of this scale. Knowledge is our first and most important tool in addressing an issue of this scale.

As we come to the end of this reflection on violence, consider this: perhaps one of the most powerful steps toward peace begins within yourself. It's time to reach out to someone you believe you've wronged—whether recently or in the distant past. Take the simple yet profound action of getting back in touch, picking up the phone, and offering an apology. Feel the weight lift as you acknowledge your humanity, a mixture of both strengths and flaws. Like lifting a long-standing curse, this act of humility brings with it a sense of liberation and empowerment. Even if the gesture doesn't lead to any outward reconciliation, the internal shift will leave you feeling lighter, more invigorated, and relieved. This small act can be a powerful first step in breaking cycles of harm and moving toward a world less burdened by violence and conflict.

4

Governance

Time for regovernance?

At its core, governance refers to the systems, processes, and structures through which authority is exercised and decisions are made and implemented. It's about how rules, norms, and actions are structured, sustained, and held accountable. Governance applies to various levels, including corporate governance (how companies are directed and controlled), public governance (how governments manage public resources and affairs), and global governance (how international issues are handled collectively).

Zooming in on public governance, it refers to the systems by which governments manage public resources, implement policies, and engage with citizens. The most common and generally accepted form is democratic governance, which prioritizes public participation, free elections, and the rule of law.

Democratic governance manifests in various forms across the globe, each reflecting the unique historical, cultural, and social contexts of the respective nations. Often, a democratic system is characterized by a parliamentary structure that emphasizes coalition-building and compromise, ensuring a diversity of voices in decision-making processes. A strong commitment to the rule of law and human rights is evident through its robust constitutional framework, which includes mechanisms for judicial review and the protection of individual freedoms.

In the United States, democratic governance is rooted in a system of federalism, where power is divided between national and state governments. The electoral system allows for significant public participation, with regular elections and a range of mechanisms for civic engagement. However, the U.S. system faces challenges, including political polarization and issues related to campaign financing that can impact the fairness of elections. Nonetheless, the country's emphasis on constitutional rights and the separation of powers remains foundational to its democratic ideals.

In any case, a democratic government should be responsive to the needs and preferences of the people, fostering trust between citizens and their leaders. In theory, safeguards exist to create a balance and allow citizens to hold their leaders accountable. Yet, in practice, they are often more fragile and susceptible to manipulation than we would hope. While democratic governance presents an ideal of inclusiveness and fairness, its effectiveness often falls short in practice. Corruption, external influences, and disinformation can severely undermine electoral processes, distorting representation and eroding trust in democratic institutions. Additionally, political polarization, particularly in deeply divided societies, can hinder meaningful dialogue, limiting the government's ability to address issues in a balanced way. In such environments, governance becomes more about partisan struggles than about responding to citizens' needs, raising critical questions about whether democratic systems always live up to their foundational principles of equality, representation, and accountability.

In reflecting on the structures and systems that shape our society today, especially democratic governance, it's important to pause and ask: are we at the pinnacle of political and societal development? Democracy, with its ideals of freedom, equality, and the rule of law, is often held up as the highest form of governance humanity has achieved so far. But when we look deeper, it's worth questioning whether the systems we have in place are as effective or fair as they could be.

There's a tendency to accept that what we have today is "as good as it gets." The complexity of modern society, the interdependence of global economies, and the challenges of balancing individual freedoms with collective responsibilities often make it seem as if no better alternative exists. Yet, acknowledging the flaws in our democratic systems—whether through political polarization, weakened accountability, or inequality—suggests that perhaps we shouldn't settle for the status quo.

Is it possible that democracy, like all other systems, is still a work in progress rather than a final destination? Instead of accepting its shortcomings as inevitable, maybe we should view them as areas that need reform or even a rethinking of what governance could look like in the future. Could new forms of political organization, powered by technology or more direct forms of citizen engagement, help us push beyond the limitations of today's systems?

The idea that democracy might be a work in progress rather than a final form opens up a significant conversation about the evolution of governance. Historically, every system of governance has evolved in response to changing social, economic, and technological conditions. Democracy, in its modern form, is no exception. The challenges it faces today—rising political polarization, the influence of money in politics, and the decline of trust in public institutions—may signal not that democracy has failed, but rather that it needs to adapt to new realities. Reforming democratic systems could mean revitalizing its core principles while addressing these evolving challenges.

One possible direction for such reform is the integration of more direct forms of citizen participation. The rise of digital platforms, for instance, could enable new methods of engagement beyond the traditional electoral cycles. Initiatives such as participatory budgeting or direct digital referendums are already being explored in some parts of the world. These approaches give citizens more direct control over decision-making, which could revitalize the connection between governance and the people it serves. This potential for innovation suggests that democracy, while imperfect, can evolve into something more responsive and representative in the future.

While it's easy to focus on the flaws and limitations of democratic systems, it's important to recognize that much of what has been achieved through democracy should not be dismissed. The freedoms many of us enjoy today—freedom of speech, freedom of assembly, and the right to vote—are hard-won gains that represent the culmination of generations of effort. These freedoms, protected by the rule of law, are foundational to the stability and prosperity seen in many democratic societies. While far from perfect, these systems have created space for human rights, social progress, and individual freedoms to flourish in ways that are often taken for granted.

Moreover, the democratic world has facilitated monumental advances in areas such as education, healthcare, and civil rights. Many public institutions that we rely on daily—from schools to hospitals—are products of democratic governance that values the public good. International cooperation on issues like climate change, poverty, and conflict resolution has also been driven by democratic states pushing for collective global solutions. There's a reason why many people, even those critical of their current governments, still regard democracy as the best framework for ensuring justice, equality, and representation.

This doesn't mean we should ignore its problems, but it would be unfair to entirely discount the sacrifices and dedication of countless individuals who have fought for the values democracy stands for. Their efforts have left a positive impact, making the world, in many respects, a better place than it was before. As we contemplate how governance might evolve, we should also acknowledge the successes of democracy as a foundation on which to build future progress, not a structure to tear down without consideration.

Perhaps more questions need to be asked about global governance.

Global governance refers to the systems and institutions through which international issues are addressed and managed collectively, often involving cooperation between states, multinational organizations, and various non-state actors. While local governance is typically more focused on immediate, region-specific concerns and driven by engagement with constituents, global governance deals with cross-border challenges that require coordinated action—such as climate change, economic instability, pandemics, and security threats.

One of the fundamental differences between global and local governance is the lack of a centralized authority at the global level.

Unlike local governments, which have direct jurisdiction over their territories and populations, global governance lacks an overarching structure to enforce rules or ensure compliance. Instead, it relies on voluntary cooperation, treaties, and diplomatic negotiation, which often complicates decision-making and implementation. This can lead to slower, less effective responses to crises, as international bodies struggle to align the interests of diverse nations with their own distinct priorities and agendas.

Many would argue that global governance has been inadequate in addressing some of the most pressing international issues. Climate change, for example, is a problem that affects every nation, but collective action has often been delayed or weakened by disagreements over responsibility, resources, and urgency. Similarly, economic inequalities between nations, security threats like terrorism, and the handling of global health crises have revealed serious limitations in our current structures for global cooperation. The problem isn't necessarily a lack of will—many countries and organizations recognize the need for action—but rather a lack of leadership, cohesion, and mechanisms to carry out meaningful, long-term change.

Why, then, does it often seem like nobody wants to step forward and lead on these drastic changes? The answer is complex. National governments are typically accountable to their own citizens, and global leadership may conflict with domestic priorities. Political leaders may be hesitant to take bold international actions if they fear backlash at home. Moreover, countries often have competing interests on the global stage, making it difficult to reach consensus on how to handle issues that require shared sacrifice or investment. Without strong, unified leadership, global governance can seem paralyzed by inaction, leading to frustration and a sense that international problems are being mishandled.

Are there any solutions?

Global governance today often reflects the power dynamics of a few dominant nations, leaving smaller, developing countries without a strong voice in international decision-making processes. While organizations like the United Nations seek to represent a broad array of countries, their leadership structures are still weighted heavily toward the world's most powerful economies. This imbalance can skew global policies in favor of wealthier nations, sidelining the interests of regions that may be most vulnerable to issues like climate change, food insecurity, and health crises.

Part of a solution might lie in making global leadership more inclusive. Creating new coalitions or revitalizing existing global forums could give emerging economies, smaller nations, and underrepresented groups more influence. This shift would not only promote equity but also lead to more comprehensive and effective solutions to global challenges. By including a broader spectrum of voices, global governance could better reflect the diverse needs of the global population, ultimately leading to more sustainable and fair outcomes.

Secondly, in today's interconnected world, technology offers unprecedented opportunities to improve global governance. Digital platforms can be used to engage citizens directly in international discussions, breaking down the traditional barriers between global institutions and the people they are supposed to serve. These platforms can facilitate participation, transparency, and accountability, allowing citizens from every corner of the world to engage in policy discussions, propose ideas, and hold global institutions accountable for their actions.

Technology also has the potential to enhance the efficiency of global governance by providing tools for real-time monitoring of international agreements and crises. For instance, digital tracking systems could monitor carbon emissions, food distribution, or conflict zones, enabling quicker responses from global institutions. By harnessing the power of modern technology, we can create more agile and responsive global systems capable of addressing complex, transnational issues in real time.

Thirdly, the concept of national sovereignty, while foundational to the modern state system, can sometimes stand in the way of addressing global issues that transcend borders. Problems like climate change, pandemics, and human rights violations do not respect national boundaries, making it essential for countries to view their responsibilities not just through the lens of their own national interests, but with a broader, global perspective. Traditional notions of sovereignty, where national interests reign supreme, are increasingly being challenged by the need for international cooperation.

To address these challenges, we may need to rethink how sovereignty functions in a globalized world. This could mean adopting more flexible approaches to governance, where nations willingly cede a degree of sovereignty in certain areas, such as environmental regulation or humanitarian intervention, in order to fulfill global responsibilities. This balance between national and global priorities is key to developing a governance model that is both respectful of national autonomy and effective at solving the interconnected challenges of our time.

Lastly, you can choose to ignore the systems that you fundamentally disagree with and create alternatives with like-minded individuals. This approach challenges the existing structures by bypassing them rather than trying to reform them. Instead of engaging with mechanisms that feel constricting, people can build new models that reflect their values—whether that's in governance, economics, or social interaction. However, it's also one of the hardest paths, as it requires a deep level of commitment, resources, and long-term vision.

This option may appear liberating because it allows you to shape your community around shared principles, free from the constraints of conventional systems. It appeals to those who believe that change from within is insufficient or that existing frameworks are too entrenched in inequality or injustice. For example, movements like cooperatives, decentralized governance models, or intentional communities are real-world manifestations of this choice. They embody the idea that alternatives are not only possible but necessary for those who feel alienated by mainstream governance or economic structures.

The challenge, however, lies in sustainability and scale. While creating alternatives may lead to smaller, self-sustaining ecosystems of governance or social order, these models often face opposition from established powers or struggle with the limitations of resources and reach. Still, this path can offer a powerful form of resistance by demonstrating that people are not confined to the structures they were born into—something that aligns with the broader human instinct for autonomy and self-determination. In this sense, the path may be difficult, but it offers regained freedom and potential for genuine innovation in how societies can function.

In any case, one should challenge the very foundations of current governance structures. Identify the systems that fail to serve people, communities, or the planet, and choose to disengage from them. One can either support or build alternative models that prioritize sustainability, equity, and community engagement, or actively participate in efforts to reform the existing systems from within. By choosing the first path, individuals and groups can cultivate innovative approaches to governance that reflect their values, creating vibrant, self-sustaining communities. On the other hand, engaging in advocacy, policy-making, and civic participation allows for the transformation of entrenched systems, ensuring they evolve to better meet the needs of society. Ultimately, the power should lie in the hands of the people, to decide how they want to engage with the governance structures that affect their lives.

Remember though that change, especially systemic change, is inherently challenging—particularly for those who benefit from the status quo. People in positions of power often resist disruption because it threatens their control, security, or established interests. However, history has shown that when alternative solutions gain traction and capture the interest of enough people, outdated systems are gradually replaced. These shifts are rarely swift; they take time, effort, and persistence. While it may be frustrating to witness how long change takes, the momentum builds over time as more people recognize the limitations of old systems and gravitate toward more innovative, sustainable, or equitable alternatives. In the end, change may not come as quickly as we hope, but it is inevitable as long as we continue to push forward.

5

Money

Money, the root of all evil?

Today, most money exists as "fiat currency," a system where money derives its value from government regulations and law, rather than being tied to a physical commodity like gold or silver. Fiat currency is supported by trust in the issuing authority, typically a central bank or government, and in the overall stability of the country's economic and political system. Despite its advantages, such as increased economic flexibility, fiat currency comes with risks. Its value is only as stable as the government and economy that issue it. In situations of political instability, economic mismanagement, or hyperinflation, the value of fiat money can collapse, leading to loss of trust and economic turmoil. Nonetheless, fiat currency remains the backbone of the global economy, underpinned by central banks, regulatory frameworks, and trust in governmental stability.

In order to survive in modern society, we all need money. This necessity goes beyond just securing luxuries or comforts—it is integral to accessing basic needs like food, shelter, healthcare, and education.

Money acts as the primary medium through which we exchange goods and services, meaning that no matter what our lifestyle or ideology may be, we are tied into the monetary system. It structures how we work, how we save, and ultimately, how we live. For many, the pursuit of money can become an all-encompassing force, shaping personal goals and even relationships. The requirement to earn money pushes individuals into jobs that they may not necessarily enjoy, just to meet basic needs. This reliance on money as the foundation for survival creates stress and economic inequality, as those without sufficient financial resources are left in precarious positions. Economic insecurity can limit access to quality healthcare, education, and pathways to move up the social and economic ladder, further reinforcing the cycle of dependence on the monetary system. At the same time, this dependence on money fuels structures that prioritize economic growth and profitability above other values like environmental sustainability or social justice. The constant push for higher profits, efficiency, and growth often leads to the exploitation of labor and natural resources. This emphasis on wealth accumulation as the marker of success overlooks alternative ways of measuring well-being, such as social cohesion, personal fulfillment, or the preservation of ecosystems.

Taking on step back, we also need to acknowledge that, throughout history, money has also played a role in advancing human progress. At its core, money serves as a medium of exchange that facilitates trade and allows individuals to specialize in different skills. In ancient times, the introduction of coinage allowed for the exchange of goods and services in a more efficient and organized way, moving societies away from the limitations of the barter system. This system enabled the development of larger markets, long-distance trade routes, and the growth of civilizations, where cultural exchange and economic prosperity flourished.

In more modern times, money has enabled the creation of financial systems that drive economic growth. By providing the capital needed for innovation and technological advancements, money has supported many global achievements, and the wealth accumulated through these advancements has helped lift millions out of poverty, improved living standards, and led to the emergence of welfare states that provide a social safety net. Furthermore, philanthropic endeavors, largely powered by money, have brought about significant social changes. Wealthy individuals and foundations have invested in global development, disaster relief, and fighting diseases like polio and malaria, positively impacting many lives. So while money has definitely been a tool for inequality, it has also been a mechanism for positive change when utilized with purpose and vision.

That being said, money has also been a source of immense harm throughout history. The pursuit of wealth, power, and dominance has often led to exploitation, corruption, and conflict on both small and large scales. The harms caused by money can be seen in various facets of society over centuries.

One of the earliest forms of harm tied to money is colonialism. European powers sought to expand their wealth by colonizing vast territories across Africa, Asia, and the Americas. These empires extracted natural resources and exploited indigenous populations through forced labor, leading to the displacement and death of millions. The transatlantic slave trade, for instance, was primarily driven by economic interests, with human lives commodified for profit. The legacy of colonialism and the wealth extracted from these regions has left lasting scars in terms of economic disparity, political instability, and social injustice.

Industrialization, while heralded for its innovations, also resulted in severe social harm. The capitalist pursuit of profit led to poor working conditions, child labor, and the exploitation of workers in factories, particularly during the 19th and early 20th centuries. Many industries prioritized wealth accumulation over the well-being of employees, creating environments rife with inequality and suffering. The rise of monopolies further entrenched economic disparity, as wealth and power became concentrated in the hands of a few.

Money has also fueled conflict. Wars have often been fought over control of resources and trade routes, with wealth being both a cause and an outcome of these conflicts. From ancient wars over fertile land and precious metals to more recent conflicts over oil, economic interests have frequently been at the heart of global unrest. The arms trade, driven by profit, continues to sustain conflicts worldwide, often at the cost of civilian lives and societal stability.

Additionally, financial systems themselves have often perpetuated inequality and corruption. In the modern era, the 2008 financial crisis highlighted the vulnerabilities and excesses of the global banking system, where reckless speculation and greed led to economic collapse. Millions of people lost their homes, jobs, and savings, while a small number of individuals and corporations profited from the turmoil. The crisis underscored how the pursuit of profit at any cost can destabilize entire economies and devastate lives.

Finally, the environmental degradation caused by the relentless quest for economic growth cannot be overlooked. Industrial activities driven by profit have led to deforestation, pollution, and the exploitation of natural resources. Climate change, fueled by decades of industrialization and economic expansion, poses an existential threat to the planet, with the poorest and most vulnerable populations bearing the brunt of its impacts.

In sum, while money has enabled societal advancements, its pursuit has also been responsible for vast harm, creating a legacy of exploitation, conflict, and environmental destruction that continues to shape the world today.

Are there any alternatives?

There are communities today where money does not play a primary role, often prioritizing alternative systems of exchange and mutual support. In some intentional communities, members live cooperatively, sharing labor and resources to meet their needs. These groups emphasize communal living, where the focus is on collective well-being rather than individual monetary wealth. Gift economies also exist, where goods and services are exchanged without a direct expectation of compensation. In these systems, the act of giving fosters social bonds and mutual aid, creating a network of support that relies on community trust and reciprocity rather than financial transactions. Another alternative is time banking, where individuals exchange services based on time rather than money. In these systems, each person's time is valued equally, allowing for a direct exchange of skills and services without monetary costs. This model promotes community engagement and encourages participants to contribute to each other's well-being. Additionally, certain religious communities operate on principles that minimize the role of money by focusing on shared living and communal resources. These communities often rely on donations or agricultural practices to meet their needs, fostering a sense of collective purpose and simplicity. There are a few examples that demonstrate how communities can explore alternative economic models, providing valuable insights into living with less dependence on money while promoting cooperation and social cohesion.

Initiatives that explore such alternative economic models are primarily local in nature, often tailored to specific communities or regions. These models can vary greatly in size, from small, grassroots organizations to larger networks with broader influence. Globally, some of these initiatives are gaining traction and forming networks that connect similar communities across borders, but forming such alliances to enhance reach and impact, allowing them to share resources, knowledge, and support, is never easy. Integrating technology can streamline processes and expand the capabilities of these systems, enabling better communication, resource management, and access to a broader audience, but despite these advancements, significant challenges remain in overcoming entrenched economic structures and securing widespread adoption of these alternative models.

Can you imagine a world without money?

Imagining a world without money opens up a radical shift in how societies might function. The core idea is that technological advancements could drive costs of production and distribution to near zero, leading to a world where goods and services are abundant and no longer primarily governed by market forces.

Peter Diamandis, for example, envisions a world where technologies like AI, robotics, and renewable energy significantly reduce the costs of essential resources—energy, raw materials, manufacturing, and intellectual property. As these costs demonetize or approach zero, society could move away from scarcity-driven economics. In a future where solar power provides abundant free energy, automated factories and 3D printers produce goods at minimal costs, and ideas spread freely across decentralized networks, money might lose its central role. People would no longer need to exchange currency for basic needs like housing, food, and energy.

Jeremy Rifkin's concept of a "Zero Marginal Cost Society" builds on this vision, where collaborative commons and digital platforms reduce the costs of goods and services to the point that they become almost free. In this future, extreme productivity driven by automation, digitalization, and decentralized technologies (such as blockchain and open-source platforms) would disrupt traditional capitalist systems. Individuals would rely less on commercial markets and more on peer-to-peer exchanges, shared knowledge, and cooperative networks for the production and distribution of goods and services. The "collaborative commons" would emerge as a dominant force, sidelining profit-driven enterprises, and people would contribute to and access resources freely or at minimal cost.

However, transitioning to such a world is fraught with challenges, as it would require a fundamental rethinking of societal structures. Governments, corporations, and financial systems would need to adapt to a new paradigm where ownership, value, and productivity are no longer anchored to money. The role of work, labor, and personal identity might also transform, with people shifting from transactional roles to more community-oriented, creative, or technological engagements.

The ultimate question becomes: If money loses its influence, what will drive people's motivation? Is competition still necessary? This post-monetary world might emphasize collaboration and collective growth over individual gain, but it would also demand new systems of governance, equity, and sustainability to ensure fair access to resources and prevent new forms of inequality.

While the idea of a money-free society remains speculative, the rapid development of technology makes this scenario not entirely unimaginable.

Would you like to live in a money-free society? It's a challenging question, one that makes us reconsider many aspects of our current lives. Imagine waking up in a world where food, housing, clothing, education, and healthcare are completely free. How would it influence your daily routine? Would you still set your alarm for work every morning, or would you stay at home with newfound freedom?

On the surface, it's easy to think that without the pressure of earning a living, many might choose to disengage and do nothing. But is that really what would happen? Humans are inherently driven by purpose, by goals, and by the desire to contribute. It's unlikely that most people would simply become passive in such a society. Many would still seek out activities that challenge them, allow them to express creativity, or fulfill a sense of responsibility. Work, in this case, could shift from necessity to passion, from survival to self-actualization.

Would some people try to take advantage of such a system, exploiting the absence of monetary obligations to avoid contributing altogether? Certainly, there are always those who attempt to cheat any system. But with the right structures and incentives—perhaps systems that reward collaboration, creativity, and innovation—this can be minimized. Moreover, without the anxiety and fear that often come with financial insecurity, people may be less inclined to disengage from productive, meaningful work.

Then there's the question of those who prefer the capitalistic approach, the individuals who thrive on the accumulation of wealth and power. Would such a society be appealing to them? Some might resist the transition, clinging to the familiar patterns of hoarding resources for personal gain. But as the idea of a money-free society gains traction and becomes embedded in everyday life, would it still be desirable to live as an isolated capitalist in a world increasingly focused on communal well-being? Perhaps not.

Ultimately, these are questions without easy answers. But they invite us to reflect on what really motivates us. Is it money, or something deeper? Would a society without money encourage a more genuine pursuit of purpose and connection, or would it give rise to new challenges? In any case, confronting these possibilities is the first step toward imagining a radically different future.

To wrap up this chapter, let's try an experiment. Pick any product or service in your daily life—a loaf of bread, a haircut, a piece of furniture— and ask the supplier what it would take for them to offer it to you for free. The goal isn't to simply get something without cost, but to understand what they would need in order to make that possible. For instance, would they need free ingredients, free labor, or free utilities? Let them trace that question back to their own suppliers—what would their flour mill, their energy provider, or their equipment supplier need to make their contribution free? Each step in the chain would require the same introspection: what would the suppliers of those suppliers need to eliminate their costs? Continue this exercise until you reach the very root of the production process, the raw materials, labor, or energy sources themselves.

The idea is to carve out how interconnected all these relationships are and to see what would truly be required to bring about such a change. It's an exercise in understanding the vast networks of dependencies that make up our economic system. Of course, asking for a free Ferrari might be more complicated than asking for free bread, but it illustrates the point nonetheless.

By exploring this, you begin to see how deeply embedded money and trade are in our society, and perhaps you'll uncover ways in which small shifts toward a different model could be made. What chains would need to be broken or reimagined? What would need to change for things to move away from monetary transactions and toward alternative forms of exchange? This experiment invites you to think critically about how even small changes can ripple through the system, and what it might take to create a world less dependent on money.

6

Nature

The impact of human activity on nature has become an urgent topic of conversation across the globe. From deforestation and habitat destruction to climate change and biodiversity loss, humanity's industrial progress has come at a significant cost to the environment. Despite increased awareness, we continue to witness species extinction at alarming rates, the acidification of oceans, and the alteration of ecosystems through pollution and unsustainable resource extraction. While environmental activism has grown in response, there are still plenty of individuals and groups who dismiss or downplay the severity of the situation, insisting that nature can cope with human presence or even benefit from human intervention.

But let's ask ourselves: Wouldn't nature be better off without humans? Consider the fact that for millennia, ecosystems thrived in equilibrium without human interference. Species evolved and adapted, relying on natural cycles that sustained balance. Now, human-driven activities have upset those cycles, putting immense pressure on planetary systems. Deforestation not only destroys habitats but also weakens the Earth's ability to absorb carbon, accelerating climate change. Pollution—from plastics in the oceans to toxic waste in rivers—chokes ecosystems that have no means of quickly repairing the damage. And while some believe humans are helping by managing resources more efficiently, the question is: how often does that management prioritize nature's long-term well-being over short-term economic gains?

On the flip side, it's true that many people and organizations are dedicating themselves to protecting the planet. Conservation efforts, reforestation, and sustainability initiatives are shining examples of the potential to correct our course. These activists work tirelessly, each in their way, to raise awareness, drive policy changes, and heal the environment where possible. But for every tree planted, there are miles of forest being cleared; for every protected species, others teeter on the brink of extinction.

In this context, we should ask: Should nature be thankful for humanity's interventions? Are we truly improving the natural world with our industrialization and technological advancements, or are we simply rearranging the pieces of a puzzle that wasn't broken before we came along? Would ecosystems not flourish more abundantly if left undisturbed by human interference? Nature, it seems, would likely fare far better without human intrusion. That's not to say humans have no role or responsibility. But it's worth reflecting on how we frame our relationship with nature. We must recognize that in most cases, nature was perfectly capable of maintaining its balance long before we arrived—and may once again if we allow it.

But here we are, having spread across the planet, leaving no corner untouched. Humanity has extended its reach far beyond what any other species has done, conquering new territories, reshaping landscapes, and exploiting every available resource. It's a phenomenon that's difficult to ignore. As Agent Smith from The Matrix movie once observed, humans differ from other mammals in that we do not develop a natural balance with our environment. Instead, we expand, consume, and move on, relentlessly multiplying until the resources of any given area are depleted. Smith compares this behavior to that of a virus, noting that like a disease, humanity spreads uncontrollably, consuming everything in its path, with no regard for sustainability or equilibrium.

This harsh reflection forces us to ask ourselves: Are we truly living harmoniously with nature, or are we a force of destruction, stripping the planet of its ability to heal and regenerate? The metaphor may be extreme, but it sheds light on our collective behavior and the toll it takes on the planet. While nature seeks balance, humanity often disrupts it, leaving behind a trail of degradation that is becoming increasingly difficult to reverse. In this context, it's worth reflecting on whether we can, or should, continue down this path—or if we can shift our trajectory before it's too late.

Smith's assertion, "we are the cure", raises an interesting question about the potential role of artificial intelligence (AI) in addressing the problems humanity has created. AI, far from a fictionalized overseer of human destiny, has the capacity to offer tools and solutions that can help mitigate many of the crises we face today. But rather than a "cure" that replaces human agency, AI might serve as a building block in solving complex challenges, particularly when it comes to environmental degradation.

One of the most promising areas where AI is already showing its value is in environmental monitoring and climate science. AI-powered systems can process vast amounts of data far quicker than humans, helping to track deforestation, predict natural disasters, and monitor endangered species. These systems are being used to better understand ecosystems and the impact of human activity on the planet, providing insights that can lead to more informed policy decisions and sustainable practices.

AI can also help improve efficiency in industries that have historically contributed to environmental harm. For example, AI-driven energy systems can optimize energy use in homes and industries, reducing waste and reliance on non-renewable resources. In agriculture, AI is helping to develop more efficient farming techniques that use fewer resources while increasing yields, which can combat food scarcity while minimizing environmental impact.

However, AI is not a silver bullet. While it offers powerful tools to help clean up the mess humanity has made, it is only part of the solution. The real challenge lies in how humans choose to use this technology. If wielded wisely, AI could play a key role in reshaping our relationship with nature, but it must be guided by ethical and sustainable goals rather than a drive for profit or control. Much like in the movie, the future depends on the choices we make—whether we continue down a path of destruction, or leverage our creations to foster a more harmonious existence with the planet.

We certainly don't want to find ourselves in the dystopian future portrayed in The Terminator movies, where AI and robots dominate the planet, leaving humanity on the brink of extinction. In that storyline, machines develop an overwhelming power, leading to a bleak reality in which a small band of rebels fights against their technologically superior oppressors. One of the key elements in the movie's plot is the characters' ability to travel back in time to alter history and prevent the rise of this terrifying AI. However, in the real world, humanity doesn't have that luxury. Time travel is pure fiction, and there's no way for us to undo the damage already done or the systems we've set in motion.

What we do have, though, is the present. The choices we make today are critical in shaping the future of AI and technology's role in society. Instead of fearing an inevitable takeover, we can focus on building ethical, accountable, and human-centered AI that enhances life rather than threatening it. This requires conscious effort, from governments, companies, and individuals alike, to steer technological development in a direction that prioritizes sustainability, fairness, and the collective good of both humans and the planet. We may not be able to turn back the clock, but we do have the power to influence the future, and that's where our focus should be.

A big thank you is certainly owed to the activists who tirelessly work to protect our planet, but the question remains: Is it enough? While protests, awareness campaigns, and grassroots movements have raised vital attention to issues like industrialized fishing, deforestation, and climate change, these actions alone cannot stop the massive depletion of our oceans, forests, and ecosystems. We are facing global crises driven by industries that operate on a scale far larger than what traditional activism can tackle alone. Awareness is just the beginning— what we need now is coordinated global action, deeper systemic change, and innovative solutions that address the root causes of these environmental catastrophes.

The time for half-measures is over. As citizens, consumers, and members of this shared planet, we must take our efforts further. Governments need to be held accountable for enforcing stricter regulations, corporations must be pressured to shift toward sustainable practices, and innovative technologies need to be mobilized to restore balance. The burden cannot rest solely on the shoulders of activists;

each of us must push for more sustainable industries, and for large-scale policy changes that protect not just the environment, but future generations. The survival of countless species, ecosystems, and, ultimately, humanity itself depends on the choices we make today. So, the question is: Will you continue to watch from the sidelines, or will you step up and demand the change that's urgently needed?

Industrialized fishing, for example, presents a complex and growing problem that threatens marine ecosystems, biodiversity, and the livelihoods of millions of people who rely on healthy oceans. The root of the issue lies in the sheer scale and efficiency of modern fishing practices, driven by technological advancements and a global demand for seafood. Large fleets of fishing vessels, equipped with cutting-edge equipment such as bottom trawlers and massive drift nets, can harvest vast quantities of fish in a single expedition. This level of extraction far outpaces the natural rate at which marine populations can replenish themselves, leading to overfishing and the depletion of key species.

One of the severe consequences of industrialized fishing is the collapse of fish stocks. Species such as Atlantic cod, bluefin tuna, and several shark species have seen dramatic population declines due to overfishing. When fish populations dwindle, entire marine food webs are disrupted, threatening the health of ecosystems and the diversity of life in the oceans. Moreover, bycatch—the capture of unintended species, including endangered turtles, dolphins, and seabirds—is a devastating byproduct of industrial fishing techniques like trawling and longlining. This not only reduces biodiversity but also wastes a significant portion of marine life unnecessarily.

Beyond the environmental damage, the social and economic consequences are also significant. Industrialized fishing often undermines the livelihoods of small-scale, local fishing communities. Large multi-national fishing operations, with their ability to harvest on a massive scale, monopolize resources and drive down fish prices, making it difficult for traditional fishers to compete. These communities, often in coastal areas, depend on sustainable fishing practices to support their families and local economies. The loss of fish stocks and increasing competition from industrial operations have left many in precarious positions, pushing them out of their traditional ways of life.

So how can we stop industrialized fishing? Maybe by targeting key points in their supply chain, such as disrupting the production of essential equipment like fishing nets. Since only a few companies manufacture these large-scale, durable nets, diminishing or halting their supply could significantly impact the industry's operations. Imagine if these net producers were bought out by individuals or groups with environmental motives who chose to cease production. Alternatively, disrupting the supply of raw materials to these companies could create bottlenecks, limiting their ability to continue providing the necessary tools for industrial-scale fishing. While perhaps simplistic, such ideas highlight how strategic interference with essential supplies could weaken the foundation of industrialized fishing.

As a word of caution, it's essential to remain strategic and operate within legal boundaries. Engaging in actions that fall outside the law can lead to significant consequences such as legal sanctions, fines, or criminal prosecution—risks that should be avoided. It serves no purpose for you to become a casualty of your own efforts, especially when strategic and lawful approaches can also yield effective results.

Where does this leave us, "simple mortals," in the fight against seemingly invincible Goliaths? The power dynamic may feel overwhelmingly skewed, but even the smallest action—a grain of sand in the gears of a vast machine—can have a profound impact. Timing and strategy are key; it's not always about the size or scale of an attack but about striking when the opportunity presents itself. A carefully placed disruption in a well-oiled system can lead to larger ripple effects than one might expect.

Uniting against a common enemy is critical, as individual efforts are often easily countered. When forces join together, whether directly through alliances or indirectly through shared goals, the collective strength becomes a powerful weapon. However, it's essential not to rush into action blindly. As history shows, every strike has its counterstrike, and if you're not fully prepared for the blowback, the outcome can be devastating. Victory requires patience, precision, and absolute confidence in success before making a move.

Bottom line: nature deserves to be fought for!

And to the naysayers out there, it's time to wake up to the truth, so take that red pill and open your eyes to the problems of this world. Your neighbor will thank you for it, along with his children and grandchildren. We must stop being selfish and start considering the lives of future generations. Each and every one of us bears the responsibility for their well-being today.

II

The Not-so-Basics

7

We Are Anonymous

From a governmental perspective, anonymity is often seen as a threat. National security and law enforcement agencies argue that the ability to track individuals is essential to prevent criminal activities and protect citizens. As a result, legislation around the world has become increasingly restrictive on privacy practices, with data retention laws, surveillance programs, and identification requirements tightening across various regions. The result is a climate where seeking to remain anonymous is sometimes cast as suspicious, rather than a basic right, making privacy a difficult goal to achieve and sustain.

Additionally, in our hyper-connected digital age, information about people is collected at nearly every turn: online interactions, shopping habits, social media behavior, and even physical movements are tracked and often recorded. This growing surveillance has sparked debate about individuals' right to privacy and the ability to remain anonymous in a world that seems increasingly determined to capture every aspect of our lives. Obviously, one of the main drivers of this loss of anonymity is the monetization of data. Corporations and governments alike benefit from having detailed information about individuals, as it allows for personalized advertising, targeted messaging, and even predictive modeling for consumer and social behaviors. Personal data has become a commodity, and companies collect it to increase profits, often without explicit consent or transparency. This dynamic turns individuals into data sources rather than autonomous entities, making anonymity harder to protect and even framing it as a barrier to profitability for some of the world's largest corporations.

But why should preserving the right to anonymity be so challenging, particularly when technology now exists to protect individuals' identities better than ever before? This tension raises critical questions about freedom, autonomy, and the right to exist outside of constant observation. The issue of anonymity isn't just a concern for activists or whistleblowers—it's a fundamental right that applies to everyone, and the right to exercise it is becoming an increasingly complex battle.

The concept of identity has roots that extend far back into human history, evolving as societies have transformed over time. In the earliest human communities, identity was likely defined by one's immediate role within a group—hunter, gatherer, healer, or leader. In these small, tightly-knit communities, there was little need for a distinct, formalized identity; people were known by their role and personal traits, as everyone interacted regularly. This local and communal sense of identity was based on direct relationships and shared cultural practices, forming a foundation that persisted for a very long time.

As societies began to expand and complexify with the advent of agriculture and the establishment of villages, towns, and eventually cities, so too did the concept of identity. Formal names, family affiliations, and symbols like clan emblems emerged to represent one's lineage and social standing within larger groups. Over time, identity became increasingly intertwined with notions of religion, land, and allegiance. Titles, surnames, and social status were deeply significant, as one's identity became associated with a broader social contract. Religious affiliation, guild memberships, and feudal systems further influenced identity, and, as states and empires expanded, the need for more formalized identification grew, leading to innovations like written records and citizenship. The rise of the nation-state and advances in record-keeping technology brought a new level of standardization to identity. Governments began issuing documents like birth certificates, passports, and social security numbers, which formalized personal identity in ways that were unprecedented.

This shift from community-based identity to state-sanctioned, document-based identity represented a transformation in how society viewed individuals, framing identity as something to be managed, recorded, and verified on a mass scale. Today, this historical trajectory has culminated in digital identities, which are both ubiquitous and complex, combining data from multiple sources to form a profile that represents individuals in the modern world.

Today, the concept of identity as something issued and sanctioned by the nation-state is deeply embedded in our lives, but it brings up pressing questions around autonomy, privacy, and the individual's role in society. Identity documents, once a tool of practicality to confirm citizenship and access rights, have become gatekeepers of individual movement, access to resources, and even civil liberties. For example, without state-issued identification, people often face obstacles accessing healthcare, employment, or financial services. This dependence on state-recognized identity can create a sense of entrapment, where individual existence and freedom are validated by the state's acknowledgment rather than personal autonomy. This reliance also becomes problematic when state identities are revoked or denied due to political, social, or bureaucratic reasons, leaving people effectively stateless and marginalized.

The rise of digital identities has brought new challenges, blurring the line between public and private identities. State and corporate surveillance, often justified in the name of security or convenience, means that vast amounts of personal information are being gathered, stored, and analyzed without direct consent. As such, the right to privacy and anonymity is increasingly compromised. When governments and corporations can monitor and influence citizens' behaviors, people may feel less empowered to freely express themselves or make choices outside the norm, fostering a chilling effect on freedom and individuality.

Further, globalization has highlighted the limitations of rigid, nation-state identities. In a world where people frequently move across borders for work, education, and safety, a single national identity can feel restrictive and outdated. As global problems like climate change and economic inequality necessitate cross-border cooperation, the nation-state identity framework often complicates collaboration. This has led to calls for more flexible, transnational identity models that respect individual autonomy, provide portability, and transcend political borders.

In sum, today's identity structures, while functional, may be failing to address the complex needs of a connected, mobile, and increasingly digital world. A new framework is needed—one that even goes beyond the concept of universal digital identities recognized globally, but not confined to a single state. This vision would put individual rights front and center, championing privacy as a fundamental right and making anonymity a cornerstone. Such an approach would guard against the pervasive surveillance currently embedded in most identification systems. Imagine an identity model where the individual is empowered to control what information is shared and with whom, ensuring that personal autonomy is protected by design. By making anonymity an inbuilt feature, this system would allow people to interact, move, and express themselves freely without the constant gaze of surveillance hindering their rights and freedoms.

The notion that a privacy-centered identity system would compromise security or enable unchecked wrongdoing is a common response, but it reveals a narrow perspective influenced by the status quo. This view assumes that the only way to maintain order is through constant surveillance, failing to imagine alternatives that could both protect privacy and uphold accountability. Furthermore, the resistance to exploring these alternatives often comes from those who benefit directly from the current systems of control and observation—governments, corporations, and institutions with vested interests in maintaining the status quo. They argue that surveillance is necessary for public safety, but this claim overlooks the fact that people have the right to privacy and autonomy over their own data. Technological advances now make it possible to design systems where identity information is shared only as needed, with options for pseudonymity or full anonymity. Far from fostering lawlessness, such systems can actually support a fairer, more transparent framework by reducing opportunities for data misuse and protecting individuals from the growing risks associated with centralized data collection.

In reality, there are other approaches to managing identity that do not involve blanket monitoring of personal data.

In our daily lives, we already juggle multiple forms of identity, tailored to specific environments. While most people rely on a state-issued ID or passport for official identification, they simultaneously maintain various other identities in both digital and social spaces. For instance, gamers often create unique personas on gaming platforms, where their identity is defined by their gaming skills, alliances, or in-game characteristics. Similarly, on social media and dating platforms, people carefully curate identities to reflect the aspects of themselves they wish to present. Even outside the digital realm, people naturally adapt their identities to fit into different social contexts—acting differently at work, at home, or in a community group. This concept, often referred to as "contextual identity", recognizes that each identity may emphasize different traits, values, or behaviors, depending on what is appropriate or expected in a given situation.

The flexibility of these multiple identities allows individuals to express themselves more fully and authentically by selecting characteristics that resonate best with each environment. It also provides a level of protection; when individuals don't have to reveal their entire identity in every context, they can avoid unnecessary exposure to judgment or scrutiny. By isolating specific characteristics that are relevant to a particular group or purpose, people gain control over how much they reveal and to whom. In this way, identity becomes something dynamic and adaptable, rather than static and singular.

Today's digital landscape, however, complicates this ability to manage identities selectively. Increasingly, systems are designed to tie all aspects of an individual's online presence back to a single, unified identity, often linked to personal information like names, addresses, or national identifiers. This push toward a singular identity system overlooks the practical and social benefits of contextual identities and increases the risk of privacy violations. By reconsidering how we use identity, especially in digital spaces, we could adopt more flexible systems that allow for selective disclosure of information, letting individuals reveal only what's relevant to each context. This would align with how identity naturally functions in society and would help protect individual privacy without sacrificing the ability to interact effectively in different environments.

Consider contextual identity as crucial for managing privacy, security, and personalization. It involves recognizing how individuals interact with different platforms, services, or devices, and tailoring experiences or security measures accordingly. This approach helps to build a more nuanced understanding of people beyond basic demographics, taking into account their behaviors, preferences, and needs in various environments.

Incorporating contextual identity into nation-state identification could allow individuals to interact with their government and society in ways that align more closely with the complexities of modern life. Rather than a singular, all-encompassing identifier that attempts to capture every facet of a person's identity for all purposes, contextual identity would mean having distinct identities relevant to specific areas of interaction. This could give people more control over what aspects of their identity they reveal, fostering both privacy and security without unnecessary exposure of irrelevant personal information.

The idea of building distinct identity profiles serves a critical function in a digital and globally connected world. Much like levels or experience points (XP) in a computer game, each identity profile gradually amasses value through accumulated knowledge, trust, and experience, often tailored to a specific purpose. For example, an individual may have a professional identity, where trust and experience are built through consistent performance within a given industry. At the same time, they might cultivate a completely separate profile on a social platform, where relationships and interactions follow different norms and criteria for trustworthiness. These profiles evolve over time, and because they become unique to their specific contexts, they gain value that a single, aggregated identity simply cannot match.

Having these distinct profiles also gives people the power to reset or start fresh when desired, which is essential in maintaining a sense of agency over one's identity. If, for instance, a professional profile no longer reflects an individual's career goals, they could choose to develop a new profile with new goals and values, free from past associations. Starting over may mean rebuilding trust, but the freedom to make that choice is empowering and mirrors the flexibility often seen in computer games, where users can restart with a new character or avatar. This choice to start anew is not simply symbolic; it offers a level of privacy, autonomy, and control that is rarely achievable in the rigid identity systems managed by nation-states. Just as in a game, rebuilding can offer new challenges and a renewed sense of purpose while leaving behind a digital footprint that no longer aligns with one's current identity.

Building trust is an intricate process that inherently demands time, consistency, and dedicated effort. Much like trust in real-world dynamics, it doesn't materialize overnight but is cultivated through dependable, transparent behavior over time. In a trust-oriented identity system, the gradual development of trust ensures that it genuinely reflects an individual's actions and contributions within a community or specific sphere.

Investing time and effort into building trust serves several vital purposes. First, it incentivizes individuals to nurture and protect their trustworthiness rather than risking loss through impulsive actions. Since trust is earned slowly but can be lost quickly, any negative behavior has immediate, enduring consequences, encouraging individuals to act with responsibility and respect toward their communities. Furthermore, the need to start from scratch if an individual chooses to adopt a new identity functions as a natural deterrent against casual changes. Switching identities would mean sacrificing the accrued benefits associated with a trusted identity.

Critics will rightly raise a flag, and warn of the risks associated with so-called reputation scores, especially when we consider their implementation in certain nations where individual freedom is restricted. These systems, often maintained by governments, can result in highly centralized and opaque scoring mechanisms. When not balanced with personal control and transparency, such scores can limit personal freedom, regulate behaviors, and introduce biases that are challenging to overcome. Obviously, this needs to be avoided at all cost.

The concept of a profile-based system, if designed with the right safeguards, can still allow individuals to accrue experience, trust, and knowledge without falling into a "social credit" framework. A crucial distinction here lies in autonomy: for such a system to avoid becoming a tool of control, individuals must retain ownership over their data, profile, and the decision to start over or change direction. Ultimately, the success and acceptance of this approach would depend on real-world testing to refine which mechanisms truly offer empowerment without undue oversight. This careful design could allow a more respectful balance between privacy and personalization, giving individuals the ability to interact more freely and contextually across various aspects of life.

In essence, a system designed to cultivate and sustain trust reflects a commitment to fostering responsible, accountable identities while respecting the individual's right to anonymity. Not only does this approach create valuable assets for each participant, but it also enhances the overall reliability and functionality of the community. By prioritizing trust over rigid reputation scores, this model allows for a flexible system where accountability and transparency guide interactions, even as anonymity is preserved as a protective measure. With these principles in place, every participant's identity remains rooted in trust and responsibility, while anonymity provides an essential layer of privacy, empowering individuals to engage securely and freely.

Perhaps, a system of anonymous, trust-based identities, fully controlled by the individual and independent of third-party oversight, could offer a compelling alternative to today's outdated systems. Such an approach would prioritize personal autonomy and privacy, empowering people to build contextual identities for different domains and maintain accountability without sacrificing anonymity. Designed to foster trust while upholding individual control, this could be a forward-thinking solution to the complexities of identity in today's interconnected world.

To close this chapter, try an exercise in exploring some of the emerging alternatives to traditional identity systems. Start by investigating topics like blockchain-based identities, trust-based frameworks, and reputation systems. Look at a variety of initiatives and perspectives, and challenge yourself to dig into the details, examining "the good, the bad, and the ugly" in each approach. Notice where these systems succeed and where they might fall short in terms of privacy, autonomy, and real-world application.

This exploration may lead to a clearer understanding of why today's identity systems—often restrictive and centralized—are due for an upgrade. Consider how a future system might look if it were designed to put personal agency, privacy, and flexible, context-based identity at the forefront. The hope is that you'll reach your own conclusion about the need for more adaptable, secure alternatives that allow individuals to engage with society on their own terms, outside the confines of today's Matrix-like systems.

Anonymity is not just a shield; it's a key to true freedom.

8

Insert Coins to Start

In a world where access to public services and rights increasingly comes with a price tag, it's worth questioning the very nature of how governments sustain themselves. Taxes are levied on nearly every aspect of our lives, from income to essentials like housing, food, and even simple daily transactions. This model of funding—designed to extract financial support from citizens for the functioning of the state—has, in many ways, come to feel less like a fair exchange and more like an obligatory toll that often disregards individual means and circumstances. At its core, this constant imposition places a burden on individuals, reinforcing a sense of obligation and dependency on a system that demands payment without allowing for true opt-out.

Historically, many might have viewed such mandatory contributions as extortion, particularly when they are forced upon those who lack the means to pay. In past centuries, heavy taxes were often seen as unjust, sparking resistance and even revolutions. Yet today, under the guise of democracy and so-called modern governance, these practices have become normalized. People have come to accept that paying for almost every right or service is simply the cost of living in a "free society," even if that freedom comes with a significant financial burden.

There is an argument to be made that this model is fundamentally unsustainable. When participation in society is limited by financial contribution, it creates a system that risks alienating those who cannot afford to contribute at every turn. An inclusive society should not enforce a pay-to-play model but should find ways to ensure access for all, balancing the financial support of the state with a structure that respects individual circumstances. Perhaps it's time to rethink what we pay for, why we pay for it, and to explore alternative models that prioritize participation and accessibility over relentless extraction.

Throughout history, instances of leaders and ruling elites siphoning a nation's wealth for personal gain are numerous, often leading to deep resentment, social instability, and eventual collapse. Such abuses of power illustrate a common pattern: when those at the top prioritize personal enrichment over the well-being of the populace, it inevitably erodes public trust, destabilizes economies, and triggers conflict or rebellion. While each era and context varies, the outcome often remains the same—exploitation leads to resistance, and unchecked greed paves the way for systemic failure.

Today, in many self-proclaimed democratic nations, the abuse of state resources has shifted from obvious personal gain to more complex forms of mismanagement and inefficiency, often driven by institutional interests, corporate influence, and political agendas. Public funds, for example, may be diverted toward initiatives or entities that don't serve the public's best interest but rather the goals of powerful political allies or corporate backers. While these actions may not always enrich individuals directly, they raise essential questions: is there a fundamental difference between today's institutionalized misuse of resources and the personal profiteering of past autocrats?

Consider cases where government spending seems more aligned with corporate benefit than public welfare—whether it's extensive military contracts, financial bailouts, or subsidies for polluting industries. Often, these decisions are justified as necessary for economic stability, but in reality, they risk prioritizing the prosperity of the few over the well-being of the many. This disconnect can be deeply destabilizing, as public trust erodes when citizens feel their taxes are supporting a system that prioritizes corporate interests or political agendas over genuine public needs.

In such systems, the misuse of resources may be justified under the banner of economic or national interest, yet it often results in an indirect but tangible form of exploitation, impacting the quality of public services, education, healthcare, and infrastructure. When citizens feel their contributions sustain a system that appears distant from their own lives and concerns, it's worth asking if today's "democratic" abuses differ meaningfully from the overtly exploitative practices of the past. Ultimately, whether through personal greed or systemic bias, the outcome remains similar: public dissatisfaction grows, trust diminishes, and the structure of society weakens under its own contradictions.

Perhaps this is again "as good as it gets"—the most functional structure humanity has managed to build so far. Yet, even if it represents the best we've accomplished, it certainly doesn't have to be the last. Just as we've innovated and adapted systems of governance, economy, and technology throughout history, we should continue to question, challenge, and reimagine the frameworks we live by today. What's critical is maintaining a forward-looking mindset—acknowledging what works while staying open to change, adaptation, and evolution, because "good enough" rarely endures.

"Staying open to change" is often portrayed as a core principle in democratic societies, but when examined closely, this openness is not as accessible or voluntary as it may seem. Many traditional systems have become so deeply entrenched in both their structure and ideology that even small reforms are challenging to achieve. These systems often reflect the interests of long-standing institutions or individuals in power, which can inadvertently create resistance to change—sometimes under the guise of preserving stability or tradition.

In theory, democratic societies should provide the flexibility to explore alternative paths, but in practice, they frequently limit experimentation. Political and economic interests, bureaucratic inertia, and public skepticism toward radical shifts create formidable barriers. Consequently, individuals or communities with innovative solutions find it nearly impossible to implement these alternatives on a large scale. When attempts are made, they often face a slow, exhaustive process filled with procedural roadblocks that stifle any swift or significant transformation.

The rigidity of these systems is partly due to a reliance on existing frameworks that have been tested over time. However, this very reliance prevents us from adapting quickly to evolving societal needs, technological advances, or economic realities. For genuine change to occur, there must be both structural flexibility and a cultural willingness to embrace new possibilities. Without these, democracy risks becoming as resistant to change as the systems it once aimed to replace, ultimately failing to keep pace with the demands of a modern world that's constantly evolving.

Are there any systems we can learn from, systems that don't rely on traditional, punitive methods but instead reward positive engagement and incentivize growth? Modern computer games, particularly those that operate on a free-to-play model, provide a compelling example. These games allow users to participate without any upfront cost and offer various incentives based on the player's level of input, choices, and dedication over time. This reward-based structure not only motivates players to stay engaged but also respects their freedom to choose how they wish to participate and progress.

In these games, a player's success isn't dependent on penalties or mandatory "pay-ins." Instead, players earn benefits, unlock new levels, and access enhanced features through their own actions and persistence. The more a player invests in the game, the more they can achieve. This approach fosters a sense of agency and empowerment, encouraging players to explore, make decisions, and actively contribute without feeling coerced. Unlike traditional systems, where rules are often rigid and penalties are used as deterrents, these games use achievement as an incentive to build loyalty, commitment, and personal fulfillment.

This model could inspire real-world systems by shifting the focus from punishment to reward. Just as games encourage skill development and strategic thinking by rewarding positive behavior, societal systems could reward constructive contributions in ways that empower rather than restrict. Whether applied to education, work, or even governance, such an approach could emphasize growth, resilience, and the freedom to build on one's own choices—a stark contrast to more oppressive or punitive frameworks.

Let's take a look at Brawl Stars, for example. It's a rich example of how gamification can be applied to create multi-layered, engaging systems that offer players a wide array of choices and pathways to progress. This game isn't simply about winning battles; it provides a deeply structured experience that lets players develop their skills, earn rewards, and collaborate with others in unique ways. Each player can explore multiple aspects of the game, from team-based strategies to solo challenges, offering a nuanced example of how varied rewards and progression paths can motivate sustained engagement.

Players can choose from different game modes, each with unique objectives and strategies, including Gem Grab, where teams collect and hold onto gems; Brawl Ball, a soccer-style mode requiring players to score goals; and Showdown, a battle royale format where the last player standing wins. Players can also select from dozens of "Brawlers," each with different skins, abilities, strengths, and weaknesses, allowing for tailored gameplay experiences and strategies. This freedom of choice lets players experiment and adapt their approach depending on their goals and current mode, whether it's solo survival, team coordination, or strategic capture.

The game also incorporates progressive elements such as ranking systems, power points, and star points. Players can level up their Brawlers, unlocking new abilities and gadgets that give them an edge in battles. The more a player invests time and effort, the stronger and more versatile their character becomes, incentivizing skill development and dedication. Additionally, Brawl Stars rewards consistency and engagement with daily events and missions, giving players a reason to return frequently. This kind of structured reward system, which prizes participation and strategic thinking, is an innovative approach that contrasts with rigid, one-size-fits-all systems.

While it might seem overly simplistic to suggest a computer game as a model for societal structures, there's actually a strong case for why the principles behind such games resonate so broadly and effectively. Games like Brawl Stars, Fortnite, and others appeal to diverse audiences beyond just children, largely because they engage players through clear incentives, dynamic choices, and meaningful progression pathways. These games offer players control, the freedom to experiment, and a system that rewards dedication in tangible ways—all features that are noticeably absent in many real-world systems. The question isn't whether we should structure society as a game, but whether there's value in the way these games encourage engagement and provide immediate, transparent feedback.

In a well-designed game, players experience a sense of agency. Unlike many rigid societal systems where paths feel predefined and feedback is slow or obscure, games offer immediate responses and multiple avenues for progression. In Brawl Stars, for instance, a player isn't locked into a single strategy or character; they can experiment and find what works best for them, and the game rewards these choices in real time. This adaptability and responsiveness could be translated into systems that allow people more flexibility in how they contribute to or interact with society, with clear, transparent incentives that recognize their unique skills and contributions.

Additionally, games are popular because they provide a sense of achievement and reward that is often lacking in complex, bureaucratic systems. Where many real-world interactions leave people feeling like cogs in a machine, a game shows players the direct impact of their actions. The popularity of these games, especially among adults, suggests a longing for systems that acknowledge individual agency and effort. If societal structures could harness even a fraction of the feedback, adaptability, and personal investment that these games inspire, we might build systems that feel more responsive, inclusive, and fulfilling for everyone. Critics may argue that games are too simplistic, but the principles behind them—freedom, reward for effort, and clear feedback—could help address the rigidity and lack of responsiveness in current societal models.

Acknowledging the addictive potential of games is obviously important, as it reveals some core truths about why they resonate so deeply with both kids and adults. Games offer an instant, engaging feedback loop and create pathways to achieve goals—whether through leveling up, earning rewards, or personalizing avatars—providing experiences that are often missing from daily life. In a society where feedback on one's progress can be slow or vague, and where many people feel disconnected from a sense of immediate accomplishment, games tap into the universal human need for progress, recognition, and purpose. This desire isn't inherently negative; it speaks to how deeply humans value autonomy, achievement, and connection, even in virtual worlds.

Certainly, we must ask why games hold this power, but dismissing them as merely "addictive" overlooks what they get right about engagement and purpose. The goal isn't to transfer every aspect of game mechanics into daily life; rather, it's to examine what makes games so appealing and translate those positive elements into real-world systems. Kids—and many adults—already understand the potential of these systems; what we can learn from games might not be a backward view but a forward-looking approach to rethinking the systems we rely on every day.

In essence, we're exploring the dynamics of public systems that increasingly rely on individuals' financial contributions, raising questions about fairness, sustainability, and the very role of the state. Historical perspectives illustrate that mandatory contributions, once seen as forms of extortion, have shifted under modern governance into accepted norms. Yet, as public trust wanes, similarities between today's institutionalized fiscal pressures and the overt exploitations of the past become uncannily apparent. We need to challenge the effectiveness and equity of the current model, which can feel more extractive than empowering, especially when citizens see their contributions benefiting corporate or political interests over public welfare.

By contrast, game mechanics highlight an alternative approach. Unlike traditional societal systems that impose rules and penalties, games reward individual progress, offering a sense of agency and accomplishment. It is therefore suggested that systems could benefit from incorporating such engaging elements, emphasizing flexibility, transparency, and personalized rewards to foster a more responsive and inclusive society. Ultimately, the appeal of these mechanics reveals a deeper human need for recognition, achievement, and adaptability—qualities often lacking in our current structures.

Let's add that exploring alternative models of governance and societal contribution—such as using game mechanics as analogies—opens a path to rethink the traditional role of government in an era of digital interconnectivity and automation. Systems that incorporate choice, engagement, and transparent, reward-based incentives could better resonate with today's citizens, who often feel distanced from the bureaucratic, rigid structures in place.

As you reach the end of this chapter, consider taking your reflections a step further. What if you could actively contribute to reimagining traditional systems through the lens of gamification? The idea here is not only to think about how elements of games—such as rewards, achievements, or dynamic feedback—could breathe new life into established structures like social security, but to record and share these thoughts, giving shape to new possibilities.

Imagine, for instance, that you're designing a system that motivates and rewards engagement, offering citizens a sense of choice and progress. How would you apply gamified elements to cultivate a sense of belonging and satisfaction in contributing to a social system? As an example, think about a decentralized rescue system that transforms the way people seek and offer help, leveraging gamification to incentivize participation and recognize contributions. Such a platform could allow anyone with a mobile device to broadcast an emergency call—whether for an accident, injury, fire, or other crises—to nearby individuals willing to assist. Instead of relying solely on traditional rescue services, this system would empower everyday citizens to step in, creating a dynamic network of responders. The gamified element lies in offering responders a multi-layered system of rewards, including rescue points to track achievements, financial incentives for tangible recognition, and the potential to unlock new ranks, titles, or exclusive privileges based on contributions and consistency. Over time, individuals who frequently and successfully assist others could even develop a hero profile, earning trust and prestige within the community. This feedback loop of achievement and acknowledgment would not only motivate engagement but also foster a stronger sense of connection and shared responsibility. By combining decentralized technology with human ingenuity, this concept reimagines how we respond to emergencies, turning moments of crisis into opportunities for collective action and meaningful interaction.

So take a moment to write down your ideas, exploring how they could challenge or enhance the status quo. Once you've noted your thoughts, think about ways to share them. Whether in conversation, on social media, or in a collaborative space, your perspectives add to a growing dialogue on how to reimagine these systems. Sharing ideas, even unpolished ones, helps create a collective vision for the future, inspiring new models that better reflect our shared values and evolving world. Your ideas might be the very catalysts needed to challenge outdated norms and ignite meaningful change.

9

Distribution of Wealth

The distribution of wealth has long been a cornerstone of economic debate, shaping policies, ideologies, and societal structures across generations. But what do we truly mean when we speak of distributing wealth? At its core, the term suggests a reallocation of financial resources in a way that aims to reduce disparities and create a more balanced economic landscape. It's a concept with deep roots in history, from early agrarian societies that practiced forms of resource sharing to modern taxation and welfare systems that attempt to bridge wealth gaps in today's economies.

In contemporary society, the distribution of wealth is most often managed through mechanisms like progressive taxation and legal frameworks. In different ways, these systems aim to support the idea that financial resources should not be monopolized by a select few but rather shared to promote economic stability and social well-being. Countries with robust welfare systems, for example, use tax revenue to fund social programs that provide support to low-income individuals, redistributing wealth to those who might otherwise lack financial security.

Yet, despite these efforts, disparities in wealth persist, and the gap between rich and poor continues to widen in many parts of the world. These systems are also involuntary, with individuals required to contribute portions of their income or assets through mandatory taxes. For many, this approach can feel rigid and restrictive, as these contributions are not actively chosen but imposed. This raises fundamental questions: could a more flexible, voluntary, or even incentivized system of wealth distribution create a sense of personal agency while achieving economic balance?

Reflecting on the concept of wealth distribution invites us to examine what it truly means to share resources equitably within society. The concept goes beyond mere financial equality; it encompasses the idea that resources—be they monetary, educational, healthcare, or otherwise—should be accessible to all, promoting overall societal well-being. The ideal here is to create a balance where basic needs are met for everyone, while opportunities for individual growth and prosperity remain available.

In envisioning a society where equitable wealth distribution is more than an ideal, we confront the challenge of creating systems that genuinely reflect the diverse needs and aspirations of the community. Imagine a system where the distribution of resources isn't merely a corrective afterthought but an integral function, designed to uplift every member and foster a shared sense of prosperity. At its core, such a system would redefine traditional models of wealth redistribution, making room for innovative approaches that actively support financial stability for all.

One example could be a modern take on Universal Basic Income (UBI).

UBI is a concept that has gained increasing attention in recent years as a potential solution to economic inequality. It proposes that a government or other central authority provide a fixed, unconditional sum of money to all citizens, granted independently of a person's financial situation, employment status, or income level, providing a consistent baseline of financial support to all members of a population. Unlike traditional welfare systems, UBI does not involve a means test or require recipients to demonstrate financial need or fulfill work requirements. The idea is to ensure a basic standard of living for everyone, giving people the freedom to meet basic needs without relying solely on employment. It would offer financial security while reducing the need for complex welfare systems.

Advocates would state that by decoupling income from work, UBI could reduce poverty, simplify social welfare systems, and foster economic stability, while potentially giving individuals more freedom to pursue education, personal projects, or entrepreneurial endeavors. Critics would argue that UBI could disincentivize work and lead to inflationary pressures, as a universal payment could increase demand for goods and services without a corresponding increase in supply. Some also question whether UBI can be financially sustainable, given the scale of funding required to support entire populations. So where does the money for this come from? The idea of funding UBI is central to its viability and has sparked a range of proposed solutions, many of which involve taxes.

Recent UBI trials have shown mixed outcomes, with valuable insights for policymakers and researchers. Finland conducted a pioneering experiment, where a number of unemployed individuals received a monthly payment of about 500 euros. The results indicated that recipients reported lower stress levels, improved well-being, and a more positive outlook on life, while the impact on employment rates was minimal. In the U.S., a similar initiative provided a small number of residents with $500 monthly. Although small-scale, it had encouraging results: recipients experienced reduced income volatility, improved mental health, and were able to secure full-time jobs at higher rates than those who did not receive the stipend. The project demonstrated that even a modest UBI can empower individuals to improve their economic standing, reducing reliance on precarious employment and fostering personal development.

The Alaska Permanent Fund Dividend (PFD) is sometimes cited as one of the most successful long-term examples of a basic income in practice. Created many decades ago, the PFD provides an annual payment to every resident of Alaska, funded by a portion of the state's oil revenues. The amount fluctuates based on the fund's performance, typically ranging from $1,000 to over $2,000 per person. This distribution model shows how a region's natural resource wealth can be shared directly with its population, effectively serving as a partial universal basic income. The Alaska model shows that UBI can be sustainably funded through the careful management of natural resources and it provides a compelling case for other resource-rich regions considering similar redistribution programs. The PFD highlights how revenue from communal assets can be used to support social equity, reduce poverty, and foster economic stability without adversely affecting the labor market.

In general, UBI remains a compelling idea for many policymakers and thought leaders. The search for sustainable funding models has caused many headaches. Despite numerous proposals, clear and universally accepted solutions have yet to emerge. Some argue that progressive taxation could provide the necessary resources but doubts persist about the long-term sustainability of any funding models put forward so far. Concerns about their financial feasibility and potential economic side effects remain unresolved. As a result, the debate continues, with no clear consensus on a reliable and scalable funding source for UBI.

As we explore innovative approaches to UBI, it might be an idea to integrate such a model directly within financial infrastructures. Rather than relying solely on traditional tax-based funding, a system that leverages collective surplus could ensure a baseline of financial security for all. This approach might involve a dynamic currency and asset transaction model, where small, automated contributions are made through daily financial interactions, subtly redistributing wealth. In this way, those with lower account balances could find their resources bolstered, fostering an environment where financial stability comes closer to everyone's reach.

Zooming in on the asset transaction part of this model, it represents a novel approach that extends beyond the distribution of financial means only, and includes a broader range of digital assets. Instead of merely redistributing money, this could integrate a variety of digital resources or "access tokens" that grant individuals the ability to acquire essential goods and services such as food, shelter, healthcare, and education. These digital assets could be thought of as specialized vouchers, but unlike the simplistic nature of traditional vouchers, they would be more versatile and specifically targeted toward addressing fundamental needs.

One of the key advantages of such a model is its ability to direct resources toward meaningful and socially beneficial purposes. In this system, individuals would not be able to use digital tokens for non-essential or potentially harmful purchases, such as cigarettes or alcohol. Rather, these resources would be earmarked for essential goods, ensuring that wealth redistribution does not simply reinforce existing consumption patterns but instead fosters a more equitable standard of living.

Moreover, this model aligns with ongoing conversations about the role of technology in shaping modern economies. Digital assets can be easily tracked, ensuring that the allocation of resources is transparent and efficient. Blockchain technology, for example, offers the potential to create immutable records of transactions, reducing fraud and ensuring that resources are used appropriately, while offering the potential for anonymity through the use of privacy-focused protocols. Additionally, with automation and machine learning, the system could adjust in real time to individual needs, ensuring that wealth redistribution is responsive, adaptive, and fair.

By redefining wealth not just as money, but as a broader system of access to key resources, society could potentially address both financial disparities and the root causes of inequality, offering a more holistic approach to wealth distribution. The success of such a model would depend on careful planning, clear definitions of essential goods, and transparent mechanisms for ensuring that resources are distributed in ways that create long-term societal benefits.

Building on the broader definition of wealth—one that goes beyond financial assets to include essential goods and services—the concept of shared resources offers an another way to address economic inequality. Shared resources, like tool libraries, community gardens, and vehicle-sharing programs, provide access to items that might otherwise be out of reach for some people. These initiatives "redistribute" value without relying on direct financial transfer, allowing individuals and communities to benefit from assets they don't individually own.

One of the more impactful models has been community tool libraries, where members can borrow equipment and tools for projects that would otherwise require a personal investment in costly equipment. These libraries reduce financial barriers, allowing more people to engage in home repairs, gardening, or crafting projects without purchasing individual tools, thus promoting sustainability and shared responsibility. Through such programs, communities make efficient use of resources, extending the life of equipment that might otherwise sit unused for long periods, which in turn reduces waste and promotes circular economies.

Similarly, shared vehicle programs offer a practical solution for individuals and families who may not be able to afford a car or who prefer not to own one. These programs provide affordable access to transportation on an as-needed basis, thereby reducing urban congestion, pollution, and the high personal costs associated with car ownership. They also encourage more sustainable lifestyles by making public transportation and shared rides more accessible.

Community gardens, another form of shared resources, address both food insecurity and community building. These gardens enable people to cultivate fresh produce and share in the harvest, particularly in urban areas with limited green space. By distributing both the work and the bounty, community gardens support people who may not have access to fresh produce otherwise. They also promote skills, healthy eating, and a sense of shared purpose, with participants often learning about sustainable agriculture and environmental stewardship.

And let's not forget about book libraries—one of the oldest and most accessible shared resources, offering knowledge and learning to communities for centuries.

In summary, by promoting collective access over individual ownership, shared resource programs help reduce personal expenses, lessen environmental impact, and strengthen community ties. They exemplify how wealth distribution can take non-monetary forms that still uplift and empower communities, creating a foundation for sustainable growth and shared well-being.

Everyone knows the saying "time is money" but less consider what it would mean if we took it literally—if time itself served as a currency. This idea forms the foundation of alternative systems, such as time banking, where individuals exchange hours of work instead of traditional money. In these systems, each hour of service is worth one time credit, regardless of the task. By focusing on time rather than dollars, these systems promote equality, as one person's hour is valued the same as another's, regardless of the service provided. This reshapes traditional concepts of economic worth, prioritizing mutual support and community over monetary gain.

Imagining time as the basis for a currency brings up an intriguing question: could a system backed by time provide more stability and inclusivity than money backed by gold or government promises? Conventional currency depends on finite resources and fluctuates with the market, while time is a constant resource available to everyone. Time-based systems suggest that communities could thrive on an economy where everyone's contributions are equally valuable, creating a financial model built on fairness and collective support rather than individual accumulation.

Of course, using time as a currency would present challenges, particularly in valuing specialized skills that traditionally command higher wages due to training and expertise. But time banking reframes these dynamics, emphasizing the value of everyone's contributions and envisioning a society built on cooperation. This kind of system urges us to question whether financial structures could better serve communities by valuing the one resource we all possess in equal measure: time itself.

Let's have a look at the Time Banks project. It's a nonprofit organization designed to facilitate and promote the concept of time banking. Time banking allows individuals to earn "time credits" by offering services or skills to others in their community. These credits can then be spent to receive services in return, creating a mutual support system where time is valued equally, regardless of the type of service provided. This model emphasizes that everyone's contributions are valuable, whether they are professional skills or everyday acts of support, such as helping with errands or providing companionship. According to recent numbers, there are over 1,000 Time Banks operating around the world. They are present in more than 60 countries and on 5 continents, engaging over half a million people who exchange millions of hours of service each year. The initiative exemplifies how an economy based on time can enhance social welfare, reduce inequality, and strengthen community ties without the need for monetary transactions.

As we have seen, the distribution of wealth is a long-standing and complex issue, often addressed through policies like taxation and welfare systems aimed at narrowing economic disparities. While traditional wealth redistribution relies heavily on mandatory contributions through taxes and social programs, newer ideas are exploring innovative, community-centered approaches. Universal Basic Income is one proposal, aiming to provide an unconditional financial baseline for all citizens, with trials showing improvements in well-being but raising questions about long-term sustainability and potential impacts on work motivation.

Beyond financial redistribution, alternative models focus on collective access to resources rather than direct cash transfers. For instance, shared resource initiatives like community gardens, tool libraries, and vehicle-sharing programs reduce personal expenses and environmental impact while fostering social ties. Time banking further redefines wealth distribution by valuing time as currency, emphasizing equality and community support. Together, these evolving models suggest that wealth distribution could expand beyond monetary assets to encompass broader resource accessibility, community resilience, and sustainable living standards.

As an exercise, reflect on the natural resources in your country or region. What valuable assets, such as oil, minerals, electricity, or water, does your nation possess? These resources are often the foundation of economic wealth, but they are not always distributed equitably among the population. Remember the example in Alaska, and consider whether a similar approach could be applied in your country. What natural resources does your nation rely on, and how could the profits from these resources be shared more equitably? Would it be feasible for the government or another body to establish a fund that distributes a portion of these revenues directly to citizens? Think about how this kind of initiative could address income inequality and offer a direct benefit to the community, especially those who may not directly benefit from the resource industries. How could such a model be adapted to suit the unique circumstances of your country, and what barriers might need to be overcome? Take a moment to sketch out an idea for how your nation's natural resources could be used to benefit its people.

Perhaps it's time to reimagine a world where money no longer divides us, and true wealth is shared freely among all.

10

Governance as a Service

Did you ever hear about "deep democracy"? It's a concept in psychology and group dynamics that emphasizes inclusivity, awareness of multiple perspectives, and the integration of all voices within a group or community decision-making process. It goes beyond traditional democratic processes by seeking to acknowledge and incorporate the experiences, values, and emotions of all participants, especially those who may be marginalized or whose viewpoints are not typically heard. Unlike traditional democratic systems, where the majority opinion usually carries the decision, deep democracy seeks to create an environment where every viewpoint, including dissenting opinions, is acknowledged and integrated. The approach emphasizes that all voices hold valuable insights and are vital for holistic decision-making, especially when addressing complex issues that affect diverse populations.

In governance terms, deep democracy suggests a shift from top-down authority structures to a model that actively involves all stakeholders, allowing decisions to emerge from a truly collective process. It introduces practices like dialogue circles, structured conflict resolution, and consensus-building to reach decisions that reflect the interests and concerns of all parties involved, rather than simply enforcing majority rule. This model aims to minimize the alienation of minority voices and prevent the social and political divides that can arise when only the majority's viewpoint is considered. For governance systems, adopting a deep democracy model could transform traditional power structures. Institutions and organizations that implement this approach would actively seek out and address minority perspectives rather than suppressing them. This model challenges standard hierarchical structures, promoting a more circular and participatory form of governance. As a result, it's not just about formal votes or policies but about fostering a culture where all stakeholders feel empowered to contribute, ensuring that even seemingly unpopular ideas are weighed and valued.

Consider that a winning vote of 51% ignores nearly half of the electorate, leading to social and political polarization and fostering resentment or disillusionment among those who "lost" the vote. These voters are left without a meaningful stake in the decisions that impact their lives, fueling a cycle of division and opposition that can strain the fabric of society. In a world where complexity and diversity define modern society, such all-or-nothing systems are increasingly out of step with the needs of citizens who demand a governance approach that listens to and represents everyone. In a more advanced society, governance should evolve beyond this binary, winner-takes-all mindset. By exploring models that include and integrate dissenting voices, we can work towards solutions that consider the broader interests of society rather than only the will of the slight majority. Deep democracy, for example, emphasizes the importance of dialogue and compromise to ensure that each perspective is acknowledged, fostering a more united and equitable approach. Such governance models aim to bridge divides and create policies that genuinely reflect the diverse fabric of society, empowering every individual to feel seen, valued, and included in the decision-making process.

Critics of inclusive governance models would argue that the complexities of incorporating diverse perspectives could lead to inefficiency and paralysis in decision-making. The more voices and viewpoints that are considered, the longer the process may take, potentially resulting in slower policy implementation and an inability to respond quickly to urgent issues. Additionally, opponents contend that striving to satisfy everyone could lead to compromises that dilute the effectiveness of decisions, ultimately leaving no one fully satisfied. There are also concerns that such systems might be overly complicated to manage, requiring significant resources and institutional structures to ensure all viewpoints are adequately heard and integrated. In this view, governance must balance inclusivity with pragmatism, with critics suggesting that too much focus on consensus-building could undermine the practical functioning of democratic systems.

But has it already been tried?

No, such an inclusive governance model has not been truly tested on a large scale or in a way that fully leverages modern technologies like blockchain, which could address some of the technical challenges of creating a highly participatory and transparent system. While there have been attempts in the form of local citizen assemblies, experimental councils, and short-term deliberative initiatives, these are often constrained by limited reach, short timeframes, or lack of influence over actual policy. Many of these efforts remain localized, symbolic, or confined to theoretical discussions without a full-scale commitment to seeing them implemented on a national or international level.

Blockchain and other decentralized technologies offer tools for securely recording votes, ensuring transparency, and potentially enabling direct participation from vast and diverse populations. However, these tools have yet to be integrated into large-scale governance in a way that could replace or significantly alter traditional, majority-rule systems. The potential of these technologies remains largely untapped, leaving the promise of a more inclusive governance model largely unexplored in practice.

The limited exploration of more inclusive governance models is, in part, due to an underlying fear of profound change. While technological challenges are often cited as reasons for delay, these obstacles are surmountable and may even be overstated. The real resistance often comes from deeper social and psychological roots. Those who currently hold power—and the systems they control—fear losing their status and influence, as inclusive governance would demand a flattening of hierarchies and a redistribution of decision-making authority. The idea of being on equal footing with all citizens, of yielding exclusive privileges, is unsettling for those accustomed to traditional power structures.

Change, particularly at this scale, is daunting for many. Governance models have historically evolved gradually, adapting to new values, technologies, and social demands. But evolution in governance, as in any domain, cannot be indefinitely postponed. The pursuit of systems that reflect the will of the entire population, rather than only that of a majority or a powerful minority, is a natural progression. Resistance may slow this shift, but the momentum of a more connected, informed society makes the exploration of inclusive governance inevitable. Evolution cannot be stopped—it may be delayed, but ultimately, governance will transform to better align with the needs of a modern, diverse world.

As we consider future solutions, Decentralized Autonomous Organizations (DAOs) present an intriguing example worth exploring. A DAO operates on the principles of decentralization, transparency, and collective decision-making, with its rules encoded as smart contracts on a blockchain. Unlike traditional organizations that depend on central authorities or hierarchies, DAOs are governed by their members through a shared, self-enforcing set of protocols. Decisions in a DAO are made through voting processes, where participants often use cryptographic tokens to vote on governance matters. This model effectively redistributes power among members, fostering an autonomous structure where the organization can function and make decisions based on the consensus of the community.

The potential of DAOs to support decentralized governance has sparked interest because they offer a glimpse into what transparent, community-driven decision-making could look like on a larger scale. By distributing control across all members, DAOs aim to avoid concentration of power, instead creating an ecosystem where decisions and actions reflect the collective interests of the group. Furthermore, because all transactions and rules are recorded on a blockchain, DAOs inherently promote transparency and accountability—qualities often lacking in traditional, centralized governance structures. This makes DAOs particularly compelling as they offer a real-world application of blockchain technology that could be adapted to address the governance needs of more complex, large-scale societies.

However, DAOs are not without challenges. Regulatory uncertainties remain a significant hurdle, as governments worldwide have yet to define clear guidelines on how decentralized governance should be managed. Additionally, DAOs are still in an experimental phase, requiring effective mechanisms to prevent misuse or exploitation of their resources. Despite these challenges, DAOs offer a promising framework for reimagining governance, especially in a world where transparency, fairness, and equal representation are becoming paramount. If you're interested in how inclusive governance could evolve, exploring the mechanics and goals of DAOs may be an enlightening first step toward understanding what decentralized, equitable decision-making could look like in practice.

As a side note, it's important not to be swayed by the negative press that blockchain projects sometimes receive. Like any emerging technology, blockchain has faced exploitation by individuals eager to take advantage of its early vulnerabilities, casting a shadow over its transformative potential. However, just as with the internet and other technological breakthroughs, blockchain continues to evolve, becoming more secure and robust over time. DAOs, in particular, exemplify blockchain's positive potential by enabling new governance models rooted in transparency and decentralized control. While setbacks are part of any innovation process, the fundamental value that DAOs can bring to governance—empowering communities to self-govern in an open and democratic manner—should not be overlooked as we consider the future of more inclusive systems.

Let's go one step further, and imagine a world where governance is offered as a service. Individuals would no longer be bound to a singular, rigid system dictated by geography or history, but instead, they could choose from a variety of governance options tailored to specific values, priorities, and needs. This concept, known as Governance as a Service (GaaS), envisions a society where governance is dynamic, competitive, and adaptable, allowing for constant evolution and improvement. Such a system offers individuals the ability to align their social, economic, and political affiliations with their beliefs, fostering greater satisfaction and engagement.

One of the fundamental principles of GaaS is choice and fluidity. Citizens could subscribe to governance models much like they subscribe to services in other areas of life. Whether one prioritizes communal well-being, individual liberty, sustainability, or technological innovation, governance systems could be designed to cater to these preferences. Moreover, the ability to switch between models at regular intervals ensures that governance remains responsive to the evolving needs of the population, avoiding the stagnation often associated with traditional systems.

Competition among governance providers would be a natural outcome, driving innovation and efficiency. Just as businesses strive to offer superior services to attract and retain customers, governance providers would work to deliver better public services, lower costs, or more innovative solutions to societal challenges. This competitive environment would encourage experimentation and reward systems that demonstrate fairness, sustainability, and effectiveness, fostering a constant cycle of improvement. Under a competitive governance model, providers would need to continuously evolve to meet the needs and preferences of their "subscribers." This would foster a proactive approach, where governments anticipate challenges, innovate solutions, and deliver results in order to retain and attract participants. The pressure to perform would no longer be driven by electoral cycles but by ongoing consumer-like choice, ensuring that any failures or missteps in governance are met with immediate accountability as dissatisfied subscribers can swiftly withdraw their support and opt for alternative providers. Can you think of any governance models today where those responsible for failures are truly held accountable for their actions?

A competitive governance landscape would also open the door to experimentation. Providers might pilot groundbreaking approaches in areas like education, healthcare, public infrastructure, or justice systems, learning from successes and failures in real-time. Transparency would be paramount, as individuals would demand clear data and evidence of performance to make informed decisions. This process could result in the rapid scaling of successful models while phasing out those that prove inefficient or inequitable. Over time, this dynamic would build a repository of best practices, enabling governance systems to converge on solutions that enhance efficiency, foster social harmony, and address the evolving needs of diverse populations. Furthermore, the financial models underpinning such a system could further drive innovation. Providers might differentiate themselves by offering lower subscription fees (formerly known as taxation) in exchange for leaner services or higher contributions for comprehensive safety nets and public goods. This flexibility would challenge traditional assumptions about the relationship between taxation and service delivery, giving citizens the freedom to select governance structures that align with their needs.

Inclusion and diversity would be another hallmark of this system. The ability to select governance based on personal values ensures that no single ideology dominates. This diversity would not only enhance personal freedom but also encourage coexistence and mutual respect among individuals who operate under different governance structures. The variety of approaches would serve as a living laboratory for understanding the strengths and weaknesses of various governance models, offering lessons that could be applied globally. Imagine a society where people of all religions, philosophies, and cultural backgrounds coexist peacefully, each thriving under a governance model aligned with their beliefs.

GaaS is as provocative as it is aspirational. It challenges traditional ideas about governance by placing the individual at the center of the system. It imagines a world where governments serve their citizens as clients, constantly striving to meet their needs rather than dictating terms. In doing so, it redefines governance as a partnership—flexible, inclusive, and ever-evolving to reflect the complexities of modern society. Of course, existing governments will probably oppose this line of thinking, dismissing it as unrealistic or even absurd. The entrenched power structures and systems of authority would have much to lose if such models gained traction. But the question remains: would we like to try this? Would you? Could we envision a world where the relationship between citizens and governance is transformed into something more dynamic, equitable, and responsive? If so, what steps would we take to make this vision a reality?

This vision of GaaS invites a deeper reflection on what governance could truly mean in a world of choice. Imagine the services and benefits you would value enough to pay for as part of a subscription. These could range from essentials like healthcare, education, and security, to more tailored offerings like access to cultural institutions, community events, or digital tools. Consider the level of quality and depth you would expect in return—would you prioritize lean, efficient services or prefer more in-depth, comprehensive solutions?

To explore this concept further, create a personal list of governance services. Classify them into categories: must-haves, nice-to-haves, and do-not-needs. For each service, reflect on what you would consider a fair exchange. How much would you truly be willing to contribute financially for the benefits you would receive? Moreover, think about the role you would want to play in governance itself. In which decision-making processes would you want to be actively involved, and where would you prefer to leave decisions to trusted experts or representatives?

By contemplating these questions, you not only shape a clearer idea of your ideal governance model but also contribute to the broader conversation about the future of governance. What would your version of a "subscription" to a governance system look like? What balance of autonomy, service quality, and involvement would inspire your confidence and trust in a system designed to serve your needs?

As we explore the potential of GaaS, the concept of postnational citizenship emerges as a natural evolution in the context of governing our society. Traditional citizenship has been deeply tied to nation-states, defined by borders, passports, and a fixed set of rights and obligations. In a globalized world, however, this model increasingly clashes with the realities of transnational identities, digital communities, and the growing desire for governance systems that are flexible and individualized. Citizenship could become a fluid, dynamic construct, allowing individuals to participate in multiple, overlapping governance systems that align with their values, interests, and needs.

In a postnational era, the boundaries of sovereignty and political allegiance become porous, with people aligning themselves to governance models that best serve their personal and collective aspirations. This shift could redefine the nature of political engagement, where membership in a state is no longer a one-size-fits-all proposition. Instead, individuals could opt for a range of affiliations, from local and regional networks to global entities that prioritize shared human rights, sustainable development, and equity. In such a system, governance would be seen as a service, with a responsibility to the individual rather than to the state, and human rights could become the foundational framework that transcends borders.

This evolution has profound implications for the legitimacy of traditional state systems. Instead of viewing the state as the ultimate arbiter of rights and justice, people may look to international human rights standards as the cornerstone of their political and social existence. In this way, human rights can become the alternative scaffold to build state legitimacy and political life. These rights, recognized across borders, offer a universal language that can unite people in their pursuit of justice, equality, and freedom, no matter where they reside or what governance model they choose.

Ultimately, postnational citizenship invites us to rethink not only what it means to belong to a country but also what it means to belong to a global community. By focusing on human rights as the foundation of political life, we can create a system where individuals are not bound by outdated notions of national sovereignty but empowered by a shared commitment to the principles of dignity, equality, and mutual respect. This is the future of governance—a future where the state no longer defines the individual, but the individual helps to define the state.

It's important to mention that this vision of postnational citizenship does not automatically imply the disappearance of countries as we know them. Rather, it reimagines their role in a world where individuals are free to voluntarily choose their governance systems. People could subscribe to multiple systems simultaneously—local and global—selecting from a diverse range of governance models that cater to their varied interests and needs. In this framework, governance becomes a matter of personal alignment rather than geographic imposition, unlocking new possibilities for self-determination and collaborative problem-solving.

As a result, new forms of "countries" could emerge, unbound by physical borders or traditional regimes. These virtual, decentralized governance systems would transcend the limitations of geography, creating networks of shared values and objectives that connect individuals across the globe. Such entities could address global challenges, such as climate change or digital privacy, in ways that traditional nation-states often struggle to achieve. They might also foster deeper cooperation on a regional or local level, blending global expertise with the nuances of local communities.

The prospect of governance becoming an adaptable, personalized, and inclusive system offers an inspiring glimpse into what the future could hold. Imagine a world where governance is not defined by the constraints of history or geography, but by the shared aspirations of humanity. A world where individuals are free to align themselves with governance models that reflect their values and where the competition among these models drives innovation and accountability. Could this be the next great leap in human organization, one where choice and freedom redefine the very fabric of political life? If so, the question becomes not if this vision will materialize, but when.

11

Automated Instructions

By now, most people are familiar with the rapid rise of artificial intelligence (AI) across virtually every industry. Whether it's chatbots assisting customer service, algorithms driving personalized recommendations, or tools generating entire works of art, AI solutions are no longer the stuff of speculative fiction—they are becoming a part of everyday life. Many individuals have already interacted with AI, whether casually experimenting with creative platforms like MidJourney or relying on AI-powered tools for work or personal productivity. The question is no longer whether AI will transform industries, but how profoundly it will reshape the fabric of society.

It's remarkable how quickly this shift has occurred. Not so long ago, the concept of widespread AI adoption seemed distant—something reserved for cutting-edge research labs or niche use cases. From the outside, the progress felt incremental. However, the debut of generative AI tools like ChatGPT and visual platforms like MidJourney marked a dramatic turning point, propelling AI into mainstream consciousness. In just a few years, AI has moved from being a curiosity to becoming an essential part of workflows and daily routines, transforming industries at an unprecedented speed.

As this transformation accelerates, few now question the fact that AI is poised to change the world in profound ways. The applications of AI extend far beyond automating repetitive tasks; they hold the potential to tackle complex challenges, optimize resource use, and even redefine systems of governance. The possibilities are as exciting as they are daunting. As we navigate this era of rapid technological evolution, the question becomes: How will we harness AI's potential to create a future that is equitable, innovative, and inclusive?

Before we continue, it's also essential to address the concerns surrounding its rapid advancement. Critics often point to the potential dangers of AI evolving beyond human control, raising ethical and existential questions. Academy Award–winning director James Cameron, for instance, has been vocal about his concerns, particularly regarding the weaponization of AI. Drawing on themes from his 1984 film The Terminator, Cameron highlights the risks of rogue AI systems— like the fictional Skynet—that could prioritize their own directives over human well-being, potentially threatening the very existence of humanity. His cautionary stance resonates with a broader societal unease about unchecked AI development, especially in the context of military applications.

The fears Cameron and others express aren't entirely speculative. As AI becomes more capable, the line between automation and autonomous decision-making begins to blur. While current AI systems remain tools designed and controlled by humans, the possibility of creating self-governing AI raises questions about accountability, safety, and ethical oversight. Cameron's warnings serve as a reminder that even as we explore AI's transformative potential, we must remain vigilant about its risks. Proactively addressing these concerns, through robust governance frameworks and ethical standards, is crucial to ensuring that AI remains a force for good rather than a catalyst for harm.

As an example, consider AI combined with technologies like satellite surveillance. Companies like BlackSky illustrate the extraordinary capabilities that modern technology can deliver. BlackSky operates one of the world's most advanced space-based intelligence platforms, capable of capturing high-resolution satellite imagery up to 15 times a day. Their system promises near-real-time analytics, providing insights within 90 minutes of image collection, and is optimized for ease of use across diverse operational environments. By integrating AI-driven analytics with such data, organizations can gain unparalleled visibility into global activity, monitoring changes and trends with unprecedented precision.

While the practical applications of this technology are vast—ranging from disaster response and urban planning to military operations and border security—it also underscores the dystopian potential of a "Big Brother" reality. With the ability to combine multiple data layers, such as economic indicators, social media activity, and geospatial intelligence, an AI-enhanced platform like BlackSky's could, theoretically, monitor individuals, communities, or even entire nations in ways that erode privacy and autonomy. This capability, while undoubtedly powerful, raises pressing concerns about its potential misuse, especially considering the possibility that such systems could already exist without public knowledge. The fusion of AI and advanced surveillance might not be a distant threat but a reality unfolding behind closed doors, hidden from public scrutiny. This lack of transparency amplifies the risks, as tools of such magnitude could be weaponized or used to control populations without their consent. Big Brother or Skynet may be much closer than we dare to admit. Society risks waking up to a world where privacy and autonomy have already been irreversibly compromised.

Another concern surrounding AI is its potential to disrupt the job market, with fears that widespread automation will lead to mass unemployment. While it's true that AI will likely replace certain repetitive or task-driven roles, history has shown that technological revolutions often create more opportunities than threats. Just as the rise of the internet and smartphones fundamentally changed how we work and communicate, AI introduces new possibilities that can enrich and expand our professional landscape. The key lies in adaptation—individuals and industries will need to embrace new skills and mindsets to thrive in a rapidly evolving environment.

Recent protests from the movie industry against the use of AI, driven by concerns about its impact on jobs and traditional workflows, are very much understandable but ultimately futile. History has shown that technological advancements, once introduced, are here to stay and reshape industries rather than disappear. AI represents a transformative tool that cannot be uninvented. Instead of resisting this change, individuals and industries should focus on harnessing AI's capabilities to amplify their creativity and efficiency. Fighting against the inevitable risks falling behind in an ever-evolving landscape. Platforms like Runway exemplify how AI can empower creativity rather than diminish it. By advancing art, entertainment, and human expression, tools like these provide solutions that range from generating stunning visuals to producing video and sound with unprecedented precision and speed. They enable creators to focus more on the conceptual and imaginative aspects of their work, while AI handles repetitive or technical tasks. Embracing the potential of this technology unlocks new avenues for growth and innovation, ensuring that industries evolve alongside the tools shaping their future.

At its core, AI is simply another tool, much like the internet or smartphones before it. These tools have profoundly improved our lives, enabling greater efficiency, connectivity, and innovation. Similarly, AI has the potential to augment human capabilities, freeing people from mundane tasks and allowing them to focus on more creative, strategic, and fulfilling endeavors. While some traditional roles may diminish, entirely new industries and professions will emerge to meet the demands of an AI-driven world. The challenge isn't resisting AI—it's learning how to leverage it for collective benefit.

Going a bit further, the rapid evolution of artificial intelligence offers an unprecedented opportunity to transcend the limitations of traditional governance systems and social frameworks. Far from being a mere technological breakthrough, AI represents a transformative tool capable of addressing some of society's most persistent challenges. The phrase "people never learn, machines do" encapsulates its essence: AI has the ability to analyze vast amounts of data, recognize intricate patterns, and predict outcomes with a precision that far surpasses human capacity. This capability could serve as a crucial mechanism to avoid repeating historical mistakes and instead foster pathways toward sustainable and equitable development.

One of AI's most compelling contributions lies in its potential to refine decision-making processes. By integrating AI into governance systems, leaders could leverage comprehensive data analysis to anticipate problems and implement proactive solutions. Predictive algorithms could highlight risks—such as economic instability, environmental degradation, or infrastructure failures—allowing policies to be designed with foresight rather than reaction. Imagine governments equipped with tools that simulate the long-term consequences of policy decisions, making governance more strategic and adaptive. Such systems could replace the current short-term thinking that often dominates political cycles.

As we know, addressing inequality remains one of humanity's greatest challenges, whether economic, social, or political. To identify, measure, and address disparities with precision, AI could be a great help. For instance, AI models can analyze employment trends to highlight wage gaps or geographic disparities in access to education and healthcare. These insights could inform targeted interventions, bridging divides that have persisted for generations. Similarly, AI could enhance the fairness of public resource allocation, ensuring that benefits are distributed equitably rather than disproportionately favoring a privileged few. In this way, AI could become a powerful ally in the fight for a more just and inclusive society.

AI's ability to learn and adapt over time could revolutionize governance systems, making them more resilient in the face of emerging challenges. As data flows in, AI-driven models could recommend adjustments to regulations or suggest entirely new frameworks to better address evolving societal needs. This adaptability would be particularly valuable in tackling global issues such as climate change, urbanization, and public health crises. Governance systems that learn and evolve could create a foundation for long-term stability, ensuring they remain responsive to the dynamic nature of modern society.

Transparency and accountability—cornerstones of good governance—could also be enhanced by AI. Tools that track the allocation of public funds or monitor policy implementation could reduce inefficiencies and corruption. Moreover, by making this data accessible to citizens, AI can empower communities to hold governments accountable, fostering a more engaged and informed populace. When used responsibly, AI has the potential to create governance systems that are not only more efficient but also more inclusive and participatory.

Yet, with great power comes significant responsibility. The deployment of AI in governance raises profound ethical considerations. Issues such as privacy, algorithmic bias, and the concentration of power in the hands of those who control these systems must be addressed with rigor. Transparency in AI design and implementation is non-negotiable, ensuring that its use enhances human rights rather than undermining them. Ethical governance frameworks will be critical to balance AI's transformative potential with the need to safeguard individual freedoms and equity.

Keep in mind though that AI should not be viewed as a panacea, nor as a replacement for human judgment. Instead, it should be seen as a tool—a powerful one—that complements human efforts to create a better world. The goal is not to relinquish control to algorithms but to use AI as an instrument for building governance systems that are more adaptive, reflective, and inclusive. Its potential to contribute to societal growth is immense, but its application must be guided by ethical principles and a clear vision of the future we aspire to create. As we stand on the brink of this transformation, the question is not whether AI will reshape our world—it already is. The real question is how we will use this tool to create a society that reflects our highest aspirations. The future of governance could be one of collaboration—between humans and machines, between communities and systems—working together to navigate the complexities of an increasingly interconnected world.

Looking at other applications, AI has the potential to extend far beyond reshaping industries and professions—it also holds the promise of altering our understanding of mortality. In the not-so-distant future, AI could play a pivotal role in combating diseases like cancer. By analyzing vast datasets at unprecedented speeds, AI can identify patterns and correlations that elude human researchers, leading to earlier diagnoses, personalized treatments, and groundbreaking drug discoveries. Technologies powered by AI, such as predictive models and precision medicine, are already beginning to transform how we approach some of the most complex and deadly health challenges.

Further ahead, AI might enable advancements that push the boundaries of human longevity, potentially bringing us closer to a form of immortality. This prospect is both promising and unsettling, as it raises profound questions about the nature of life and the ethical implications of extending it indefinitely. Yet, for future generations, such break-throughs could become a new reality. By integrating AI with fields like biotechnology and neuroscience, we might unlock solutions to age-related decline and cellular deterioration, fundamentally altering the human experience. While the journey toward such advancements is fraught with challenges, it also represents a transformative opportunity to redefine what it means to live a full and healthy life.

While contemplating immortality, AI introduces another revolutionary concept: the creation of AI twins. In the very near future, it will become possible to generate digital replicas of ourselves—complete with our physical appearance, mannerisms, speech patterns, and even our unique knowledge base. These AI twins could preserve not just the essence of who we are but also our accumulated wisdom and experiences, enabling our descendants to engage with a version of us long after we've passed away. Imagine future generations having the ability to ask their great-grandparents for advice, share stories, or gain insights into a bygone era—all through a highly realistic digital interaction.

The implications of this technology are profound. It offers an unprecedented opportunity to preserve human knowledge and cultural heritage in a way that transcends traditional records like books, photographs, or videos. An AI twin doesn't just document; it interacts, learns, and evolves, offering a dynamic bridge between the past and the present. For educators, mentors, and innovators, this means their insights and teachings can continue to inspire and guide for generations. However, as with any powerful tool, the ethical dimensions of creating AI twins—privacy, consent, and the potential misuse of such digital replicas—will need to be carefully navigated. Still, the prospect of digitally preserving human essence marks a paradigm shift in how we think about legacy, memory, and the continuation of human knowledge.

Building upon the idea of AI twins, the concept of transferring human consciousness into new bodies, as depicted in the Altered Carbon television series, represents an even more radical vision of preserving and extending human existence. In this futuristic world, consciousness is digitized and stored in a "cortical stack," allowing individuals to transfer their essence between physical forms, or "sleeves." This technology redefines mortality, making death less a permanent end and more a logistical hurdle, contingent on access to new bodies. While this idea is deeply rooted in science fiction, it invites intriguing questions about the potential of future technologies to transcend biological limitations.

While such a future remains highly speculative, of course, it reminds us of the ever-shifting boundaries between imagination and reality. The rapid progress of AI, neuroscience, and biotechnology might one day unlock possibilities that seem fantastical today. Whether or not humanity ever achieves such a state of digital immortality, the concept serves as a compelling thought experiment, encouraging us to reflect on the essence of identity, mortality, and the role of technology in shaping our future. Who knows—what feels like science fiction now might someday become part of the human experience.

To conclude, As AI rapidly becomes a mainstream force shaping our world, the opportunities it brings are too exciting to ignore. From simplifying everyday tasks to unlocking creativity and pushing the boundaries of human potential, AI is redefining how we live, work, and imagine the future. The best way to prepare for this transformative era is to dive in—explore, experiment, and embrace the incredible range of AI tools already at your fingertips. Whether you're looking to boost productivity, learn something new, or create in ways you never thought possible, there's an AI solution waiting for you. The world is changing, and those who take the leap today will be the pioneers of tomorrow's possibilities. Don't hesitate—step into the future and discover what AI can do for you.

A new life awaits us all.

12

Next Nature Food

The global population is projected to surpass 9 billion by 2050, necessitating a substantial increase in food production. Meeting this demand without exhausting finite natural resources presents a monumental challenge. Current agricultural practices, reliant on intensive resource use and monoculture cropping, are unsustainable in the long term, risking food shortages if innovation and sustainable strategies are not urgently adopted.

The challenge of feeding all those people by 2050 while safeguarding the planet's ecosystems is a monumental task. Agriculture already dominates a huge chunk of the world's vegetated land, consumes immense freshwater resources, and contributes a large part of global greenhouse gas emissions. Despite these impacts, hundreds of millions of people are undernourished, illustrating the disparity in food accessibility and affordability.

To bridge the gap, transformative shifts in how food is produced, distributed, and consumed are essential. Increasing yields on existing farmland through sustainable intensification methods can help meet growing demand without expanding agricultural land use. At the same time, practices such as agroforestry, crop diversification, and precision agriculture can minimize environmental degradation. Coupled with efforts to eliminate food waste, improve equitable access, and support smallholder farmers, these strategies provide a pathway toward feeding a growing global population while reducing the strain on the planet's finite resources and addressing the intertwined issues of poverty, habitat loss, and pollution.

Drawing from the April 2021 United Nations report "Population, Food Security, Nutrition, and Sustainable Development", several recommendations were made for governments to tackle the intertwined challenges of food security, malnutrition, and sustainable development. These suggestions outline potential pathways forward, while also revealing significant hurdles to implementation.

Governments are encouraged to develop policies that incentivize healthy, sustainable diets and discourage those with high environmental costs. By subsidizing nutritious, eco-friendly foods and imposing taxes on high-emission products like red meat, shifts in production and consumption could be achieved. Education campaigns and school programs could further shape healthier eating habits. However, these measures face resistance from powerful food and agricultural lobbies, as well as the challenge of making sustainable diets affordable for lower-income populations.

Nutrition education could also be integrated into broader social programs, such as those targeting food security, healthcare, and reproductive health. This holistic approach could equip communities with the knowledge to make healthier dietary choices. Yet, achieving this integration requires coordination across sectors and significant resources, especially in regions where infrastructure and funding are limited.

The report emphasizes the dual challenge of addressing malnutrition in all its forms—from undernourishment to the growing problem of obesity. Governments must focus on ensuring equitable access to balanced diets that meet both challenges simultaneously. However, the stark contrasts between the needs of wealthier and poorer countries make it difficult to apply one-size-fits-all solutions, requiring highly localized and tailored approaches.

Increasing incomes among the poor is presented as a vital step in enhancing access to nutritious food. Measures such as job creation, income supplements, and other poverty alleviation programs are proposed. Yet, these solutions are deeply dependent on political stability and economic resilience. Furthermore, structural inequalities and corruption could prevent these benefits from reaching those who need them most.

Efforts to tackle food insecurity must prioritize vulnerable populations such as women, youth, and the elderly. Tailored interventions—like improving access to credit, land, and education—can empower these groups. However, deeply ingrained social norms and cultural barriers often resist change, requiring substantial investment in both policy and advocacy to ensure these initiatives take root effectively.

The report also calls for strengthening humanitarian aid systems to address hunger in crisis-affected regions while building resilience in local food systems. While this dual strategy could mitigate immediate needs and foster long-term sustainability, logistical challenges and political instability in many regions make effective implementation a significant hurdle.

Lastly, the report urges governments to ensure that global trade rules for food and agriculture account for social and environmental impacts. This would help prevent wealthier nations and large corporations from undermining the competitiveness of countries with stricter sustainability standards. However, securing international consensus on such trade policies is a complex endeavor, often hampered by conflicting economic interests and corporate lobbying.

While the UN report tries to outline a comprehensive framework for addressing food security and sustainability, it must be clear that it comes with immense challenges. The claim that coordinated global action, significant investment, and innovative solutions are sufficient to address the complex challenges of feeding the population by 2050 deserves closer examination. While these are undeniably crucial components, they may not fully account for the political, social, and economic intricacies that shape global food systems.

Firstly, coordinated global action presumes a level of international agreement and cooperation that is exceedingly difficult to achieve in practice. Diverging national interests, geopolitical tensions, and the dominance of powerful agribusiness lobbies often hinder collective efforts. For instance, trade disputes or protectionist policies can undermine the equitable distribution of resources necessary for global food security. Furthermore, efforts to align sustainability standards globally might face pushback from countries that rely on less sustainable agricultural practices to maintain economic stability.

Significant investment, though essential, also faces limitations. Funding must be sustained over decades and allocated effectively, often in regions with weak governance structures and limited institutional capacity. Corruption, inefficiency, and mismanagement can dilute the impact of even the most well-intentioned financial aid. Moreover, prioritizing investment in high-tech solutions, such as genetically modified crops or precision agriculture, risks excluding low-tech, community-driven initiatives that may be more accessible to smallholder farmers, who form the backbone of food production in developing nations.

Innovative solutions, while inspiring, are not immune to scalability and accessibility challenges. Technologies like vertical farming, lab-grown meat, or AI-driven precision agriculture remain expensive and predominantly confined to wealthier nations. Bridging this technological divide requires a redistribution of resources and knowledge that may not be feasible given current economic and political structures.

Finally, broader systemic issues add layers of complexity that cannot be easily resolved through isolated efforts. Climate impacts, for example, disproportionately affect regions already struggling with food insecurity, aggravating existing vulnerabilities and requiring solutions that are as adaptive as they are transformative.

In light of these challenges, it is important to question whether such proposed strategies will be sufficient or if a more radical rethinking of global priorities and power structures is urgently needed.

So are we doomed? Probably.

In addressing the challenges of global food security, one might wonder if we're focusing on the wrong things. While innovation often takes center stage, are these technological advancements truly solving the problems they aim to address, or are they merely expensive distractions from more fundamental issues?

Take lab-grown meat, for instance. This technology, which involves growing "meat" from animal cells in a lab rather than on a farm, has captured significant attention in recent years. It promises to revolutionize the food industry by reducing reliance on traditional livestock farming. But is this truly the pathway we want to follow?

Lab-grown meat, also known as cultured meat, is a form of meat produced by culturing animal cells in a controlled environment outside the body of an animal. Unlike traditional meat, which requires raising and slaughtering animals, lab-grown meat is created by extracting a small sample of animal cells—typically muscle or stem cells—and placing them in a nutrient-rich culture medium. This medium contains the essential components needed for cells to grow and divide. The process begins with isolating the initial cells, which are then multiplied in bioreactors—essentially large tanks designed to mimic the conditions inside an animal's body. Over time, these cells can be differentiated into muscle tissue, forming the structure and texture that should resemble conventional meat. To enhance the realism of the product, techniques like scaffolding are used, providing a framework for cells to grow in a way that mimics the three-dimensional structure of muscle fibers. This alternative type of meat is then typically still mixed with plant-based ingredients to improve its texture and flavor, resulting in a hybrid product that might feel neither here nor there. It begs the question: is the average consumer truly looking forward to eating something that sits at the intersection of lab science and processed plant food? And how nutritional is all this?

Advocates for lab-grown meat highlight several potential benefits.

It could reduce the environmental footprint of traditional livestock farming, which is a significant contributor to greenhouse gas emissions, deforestation, and water consumption. It may also alleviate ethical concerns by reducing the need to kill animals and mitigate public health risks by avoiding issues like antibiotic resistance and animal-transmitted infections.

However, there are notable challenges. The technology is still in its infancy, making production costly and energy-intensive. Scaling up to meet global demand while maintaining affordability and quality remains a significant hurdle. Additionally, some critics question whether lab-grown meat addresses root issues in the global food system, such as resource inequity or over-reliance on animal-based diets. These complexities raise the question: is lab-grown meat a true solution, or does it represent a costly detour in our quest for sustainable food systems? The fact that many startups in this space have made bold promises and sweeping claims over the past few years—only to fall short of delivering tangible results—has further undermined confidence and failed to steer the movement in the right direction. And amidst all these promises, a crucial question remains: has it already been proven that these lab-grown cells are not cancerous?

Then, why not stay with vegan food? It seems like a straightforward solution—ditch meat altogether and embrace plant-based alternatives. And yes, on the surface, that could be a viable pathway. However, before jumping to conclusions, one should take a closer look at how these vegan products are made and what they are made of. There are many different kinds of vegan meat substitutes on the market, but quite a few rely on ingredients such as extruded soy and methylcellulose.

Extruded soy starts as a natural product—soybeans—that is first turned into a powder. This is then subjected to a highly artificial process, involving high pressure and extreme temperature fluctuations. These conditions are so intense that they almost cause the material to "explode" before it's cooled and transformed into a paste. Yet, this is far from the final product. The paste still requires grinding and several days of marinating to develop a texture that resembles meat. All of this to create something that is marketed as a meat alternative. To shape these extruded soy chunks into a recognizable burger patty, an additional adhesive ingredient is necessary, as the chunks don't naturally bind together. Since egg is not an option for vegan products, many manufacturers turn to methylcellulose, a synthetic compound derived from plant cellulose, commonly used as a thickener and binder in vegan products. What's concerning is that methylcellulose is also found in products such as wallpaper glue. Yes, the same compound is used to bind materials in construction—and it's being included in food products marketed as alternatives to natural meat. To finish off this wonderful recipe, all sorts of flavors are added to make the product taste like whatever the manufacturer desires. This, in combination with the highly processed soy and binders, creates a product that bears little resemblance to its natural origins. So, is this really what the population should be eating? A product made from an array of processed ingredients, designed to mimic meat but lacking the simplicity and wholesomeness of real food?

Perhaps it's time to rethink our approach and return to simplicity. Instead of relying on artificial meat alternatives and exotic products shipped from halfway around the globe, why not focus on what's grown locally and sustainably? Local fruit and vegetables, ethically farmed meat, and responsibly caught fish offer a much more direct, natural approach to food. Do we really need strawberries in winter or beef from Japan in Europe? And what about farmed salmon from Scotland—

does the environmental cost of such practices justify the demand? We should seriously question whether this constant quest for variety and convenience is really serving us in the long run, or if it's time to reconnect with what's truly sustainable.

Will this solve the issue of a rapidly growing world population?

The truth is, there's no clear answer. Just as the question of whether lab-grown or plant-based meat alternatives will be the solution remains uncertain. As we search for answers, we're confronted with more questions than solutions, and the complexity of global food systems only deepens. The real challenge lies not in finding a one-size-fits-all solution, but in rethinking the very systems that got us here—challenging our reliance on industrial agriculture, the global supply chains that stretch across continents, and the unsustainable practices that have shaped our modern diets. We need to reconsider the foundational structures of how we produce, consume, and value food. The true solution lies not in more complexity, but in embracing simplicity, sustainability, and a return to more localized, ethical food systems that put long-term well-being over short-term convenience.

At the same time, before even considering how to feed a rapidly increasing population, we should also ask how it's still possible to feed ourselves in a healthy way. The foundations of our food systems—air, water, and soil—are under immense pressure from decades of industrial practices and human intervention. Fertilizers and pesticides seep into waterways, contaminating the very resources we depend on for life. Soil, once rich and fertile, is being degraded at an alarming rate, stripped of its nutrients by monoculture farming and overexploitation. Even the air we breathe is compromised, as agricultural emissions contribute to pollution and climate change, creating a vicious cycle that undermines the sustainability of our food production systems.

This degradation isn't just an environmental issue; it's a direct threat to human health. When soil loses its vitality, the crops it produces are less nutritious, lacking the essential vitamins and minerals we need. Polluted water supplies jeopardize not only irrigation but also drinking water, affecting communities far removed from the source of contamination. Air pollution from intensive livestock farming and large-scale crop production has been linked to respiratory diseases and other health problems, making the food we grow increasingly disconnected from the idea of health and well-being.

If these basic building blocks—air, water, and soil—are failing us, how can we hope to provide truly nourishing food, let alone feed billions more people in the future? The waste left behind by the food industry only exacerbates these challenges, with chemicals, packaging, and unused food piling up in landfills or leaching back into ecosystems. How on earth can we sustain ourselves, let alone a growing global population, if we continue to poison the very elements that sustain life? It's a question that demands urgent action, challenging each of us to reconsider not just what we eat, but the entire system that brings food to our tables.

So, what do you eat? Do you think about what you put in your mouth on a daily basis—the origins, the processes, the impact? In a world where food production has become increasingly complex, where labels often obscure more than they reveal, and where convenience often trumps nutrition, how much do you really consider the implications of your choices?

Steve Jobs once said, "Eat your food as your medicines. Otherwise, you have to eat medicines as your food." A powerful reminder, yet easier said than done. In the hustle of daily life, with countless options and distractions, making intentional and informed food choices can feel overwhelming.

Perhaps the first step in addressing the challenges of feeding the world starts not with sweeping global reforms, but with personal accountability—with each of us asking, every day: what am I really eating, and what does it mean for me, my community, and the planet?

<h1 style="text-align:center">13</h1>

<h1 style="text-align:center">Mission Impossible</h1>

The first Space Age, spanning roughly from the late 1950s to the 1970s, was defined by a fervent race between global superpowers, primarily the United States and the Soviet Union, to assert technological dominance in the cosmos. Triggered by the launch of the world's first artificial satellite, this era marked humanity's initial leap beyond Earth's boundaries. The ensuing space race saw an unprecedented mobilization of resources, ingenuity, and national pride, driven by Cold War rivalries rather than purely scientific curiosity.

Landmark achievements from this period included the first manned orbit in 1961, the historic Moon landing in 1969, and the development of groundbreaking space technologies such as reusable capsules and powerful propulsion systems. These accomplishments symbolized human ingenuity but also reflected geopolitical tensions. The first Space Age wasn't solely about exploration; it was a statement of power, where success in space symbolized broader dominance on Earth. However, with the end of the Apollo program and shifting political priorities, this era waned, leaving behind a legacy of awe-inspiring achievements and satellite technologies that would become foundational for modern communication, navigation, and observation.

At the same time, the first Space Age was also a profound source of inspiration that captured the imagination of people across the globe. This fascination with space exploration permeated culture and aesthetics, influencing everything from fashion to architecture. Designers embraced futuristic motifs, creating clothing and accessories that echoed astronaut suits and spacecraft. The era's fascination with the cosmos also found expression in architecture and interior design, and popular media reflected the cosmic allure with iconic films like 2001: A Space Odyssey and television series like Star Trek exploring the infinite possibilities of space. In essence, the first Space Age not only propelled humanity into the cosmos but also sparked a cultural renaissance that celebrated the boundless potential of human creativity and exploration.

Fast-forward to the early 21st century, and humanity is now firmly in the midst of a second Space Age, but this one looks remarkably different. Where the first was dominated by governments and national space agencies like NASA and the USSR's space program, the second is spearheaded by private enterprises, billionaire entrepreneurs, and collaborative international ventures. Companies like SpaceX, Blue Origin, and Virgin Galactic have transformed space from a battleground for geopolitical supremacy into an arena for commercial opportunity and visionary ambitions.

This new era emphasizes technological innovation, with reusable rockets, plans for interplanetary colonization, and burgeoning industries like space tourism and asteroid mining. SpaceX's development of the Falcon 9 rocket and its mission to Mars are emblematic of this shift, as is the emergence of national players like China and India staking their claims in space exploration. The second Space Age has also democratized access to space to some extent, enabling smaller countries and even private universities to launch satellites through affordable programs like SpaceX's rideshare missions.

Yet, while it promises thrilling possibilities, this era is also marked by criticism. Critics argue that the billions being funneled into manned Mars missions and lunar bases could be better spent addressing urgent crises here on Earth, from climate change and resource depletion to growing inequality. The second Space Age is both a testament to human ambition and a reflection of societal priorities, raising profound questions about whether we are solving problems or simply escaping them.

Let's look at some numbers. In 2023, global government spending on space programs reached an unprecedented $117 billion, underscoring the escalating investments in exploring the final frontier. Unsurprisingly, the United States accounted for the lion's share, dedicating a staggering $73.2 billion to its space initiatives. This level of investment highlights the U.S.'s commitment to maintaining dominance in space exploration, bolstered by programs from NASA, defense-related activities, and partnerships with private space companies like SpaceX. Trailing behind, China allocated over $14 billion to its ambitious space programs, reflecting its growing aspirations to challenge the U.S. in the new Space Age.

The space sector's financial impact extends far beyond government expenditures, of course. According to the Space Foundation, the global space economy reached a staggering $570 billion in 2023, reflecting a 7.4% increase from the previous year's $531 billion. This growth aligns with the industry's five-year compound annual growth rate

(CAGR) of 7.3%, and the space economy has nearly doubled in size compared to a decade ago. These figures highlight the expansive role of the commercial space sector, encompassing infrastructure, support industries, and a wide array of space-related products and services, from satellite communications to space tourism. Interestingly, in the Space Foundation's report, the total public sector investment in space programs is estimated at $197.8 billion in 2023—far exceeding the previously cited $117 billion. In a nutshell, the global space economy has exceeded $300 billion annually since 2012.

This immense financial commitment to space exploration and development contrasts sharply with global efforts to address pressing issues here on Earth. For instance, at the COP29 climate talks, rich nations pledged $300 billion annually to combat climate change—a sum that, while significant, pales in comparison to the projected needs of over $1 trillion annually sought by developing nations. The pledge has been criticized as insufficient, with many arguing it fails to adequately address the complexity and urgency of the climate crisis. This juxtaposition invites reflection on humanity's priorities. While space exploration undeniably fuels technological innovation, inspires global collaboration, and opens up new economic frontiers, the allocation of its resources raises many ethical questions.

Consider, too, that global military expenditure in 2023, as reported by the SIPRI Military Expenditure Database, amounts to a staggering $2,443.37 billion, with the United States alone accounting for $943.24 billion of this total. To put this into perspective, governments around the globe spent approximately $6.7 billion a day on military activities. This means that the $300 billion annual climate finance target equates to just 45 days of global military spending.

All this leads to wonder if a proportion of these astronomical amounts shouldn't be redirected to mitigate the existential threats posed by climate change, which jeopardize ecosystems and livelihoods worldwide? And shouldn't we be cleaning up our mess here on Earth first, before starting to mess up other things outside of our planet? Space exploration, while awe-inspiring, carries the risk of replicating the same patterns of exploitation and environmental neglect that have plagued our home planet. Space debris is already becoming a significant problem in Earth's orbit, with thousands of defunct satellites and fragments posing risks to operational systems and future missions. If we cannot manage sustainability on our own planet, how can we hope to act responsibly in the uncharted territories of the cosmos?

Moreover, the pursuit of space exploration often overlooks immediate human needs. Millions still lack access to clean water, proper healthcare, and education—problems that could benefit greatly from the redirection of even a fraction of the resources currently poured into space programs (and the military industry). It is not an argument against exploring the universe but a call for balance, urging us to prioritize the pressing issues of survival and justice on Earth while approaching outer space with the humility and responsibility it demands.

Despite these concerns, it is however also important to acknowledge the significant contributions the space industry can make to life on Earth. Advances in satellite technology, for instance, play a pivotal role in addressing environmental challenges and improving global infrastructure. Satellites can provide critical data for monitoring deforestation, tracking wildlife populations, and studying climate change in real time. This information enables scientists and policymakers to make informed decisions about conservation efforts and sustainable practices, offering hope for mitigating humanity's impact on the natural world.

Additionally, space technologies have revolutionized disaster management. Earth observation satellites can help predict and monitor natural disasters such as hurricanes, floods, and wildfires, allowing for more effective evacuation plans and resource allocation. These systems also support humanitarian efforts in remote and conflict-stricken areas, providing communication networks and mapping tools that save lives. Such applications illustrate how investments in space can translate into tangible benefits for the planet and its inhabitants.

Space exploration has also catalyzed the development of green technologies. Innovations like solar panels, originally designed to power spacecraft, have become a cornerstone of renewable energy on Earth. Water purification systems developed for astronauts are now used in areas with limited access to clean water. These advancements demonstrate how the pursuit of space can serve as a testing ground for sustainable solutions that address critical needs on our planet.

Moreover, studying other celestial bodies provides insights into Earth's vulnerabilities. Research on Mars, for example, helps us understand the long-term effects of environmental degradation and climate change, offering lessons on how to prevent similar fates here. Space exploration does encourage humanity to think globally, to consider the fragility of our biosphere, and to adopt a stewardship mindset—essential qualities if we are to safeguard the future of life on Earth.

In this way, while the space industry must be scrutinized for its priorities, it also holds the potential to be a valuable partner in creating a more sustainable and equitable world.

What is a growing concern, and one of the more controversial aspects of the industry, is the militarization of space. Military satellites, for example, are widely deployed and serve various purposes, including intelligence gathering, communications, navigation, and missile guidance. Countries like the United States, Russia, and China have extensive military satellite networks, some of which are integral to modern warfare. For instance, the U.S. GPS system, indispensable for civilian navigation and logistics, was initially developed for military use and remains critical for military operations. Similarly, reconnaissance satellites provide real-time intelligence on troop movements, missile launches, and infrastructure, enabling precise military strategies.

The concept of "space weapons" is a more contentious issue. While no country officially admits to deploying such systems, the technology and intentions behind certain initiatives suggest that space weaponization is a real and evolving threat. Examples include anti-satellite (ASAT) weapons, which are designed to disable or destroy satellites in orbit. Both China and Russia have demonstrated ASAT capabilities, with China, India, Russia, and the U.S. having successfully shot down their own satellites to demonstrate their ASAT capabilities in a show of force. These weapons pose a significant risk not only to global security but also to the sustainability of space, as they can create debris fields that endanger all space activities.

Then there are speculative concepts like "rods from God", a kinetic bombardment system involving tungsten rods launched from orbit to strike targets on Earth with immense force, that have been discussed in military circles. Although these have not been deployed—as far as we know—they highlight the potential for space-based weapons to become a reality and their mere consideration underscores how precarious the situation could become. The existence of even one such system in the wrong hands could escalate tensions beyond control, proving how fragile the line is between the exploration of space for progress and its exploitation for destruction.

The main conclusion that can be drawn is that while space exploration offers exciting possibilities for advancing technology and addressing pressing challenges on Earth, it also carries significant moral and strategic dilemmas. The growing involvement of private companies and the escalating investments in space programs contrast sharply with the urgent issues we face here on Earth, such as climate change, inequality, and the degradation of our environment. So while the second Space Age holds tremendous promise, it is crucial that we approach it with caution, ensuring that it serves humanity's long-term interests rather than short-term ambitions or military dominance. The balance between progress and responsibility must be carefully navigated to ensure that space exploration contributes to solving the problems of our world, rather than making them worse.

As citizens in a still very traditional society, our most powerful tool is our voice. We may not be able to directly influence the vast machinery of space exploration, but we can engage in the broader conversation about its ethical and social implications. By writing, discussing, and sharing information on platforms accessible to all, we contribute to shaping the policies that govern space and technology. Our voices can ensure that these endeavors are not driven solely by military or commercial interests but are aligned with human rights, environmental sustainability, and peace.

In a world where the power to innovate and explore is often concentrated in the hands of a few, our responsibility lies in maintaining a vigilant, informed presence in the conversation. Instead of resorting to destructive tactics or undermining progress, we must focus on building solutions—solutions that are thoughtful, inclusive, and just. The challenge is not to halt progress but to guide it in a direction that benefits humanity as a whole, ensuring that as we reach for the stars, we don't forget the ground we stand on.

Perhaps, for now, it's time to put the dream of colonizing Mars on hold. Instead of looking to conquer other planets, let's focus on preserving the one we call home. The future of space exploration holds incredible potential, but it should not come at the cost of our planet's well-being. If we are to reach for the stars, we must first learn how to live harmoniously here on Earth—ensuring that our advancements in space are not only a testament to human ingenuity but also to our capacity for stewardship, compassion, and responsibility. Only then can we truly say we are ready to venture beyond our world, not as conquerors, but as mindful explorers.

14

Electric Sheep

The story of electricity's evolution starts a long time ago, beginning with early observations in ancient civilizations. Greek philosophers, as early as 600 BCE, discovered static electricity by rubbing amber (the Greek word for which is electron) against materials like fur, noticing it could attract light objects. These early experiments laid the groundwork for understanding electrical phenomena, though practical applications were far from realized. During the Renaissance and Enlightenment periods, experiments with electricity gained momentum, and by the 17th and 18th centuries, devices capable of generating and storing electricity emerged. These tools allowed scientists to explore electric currents and sparks systematically, a key step that opened the door to harnessing its potential for more complex applications.

The 19th century ushered in groundbreaking developments as electricity shifted from experimental curiosities to a practical energy source. Key figures like Michael Faraday and James Clerk Maxwell laid a foundation for understanding electromagnetism, with Faraday's invention of the electric dynamo marking a pivotal moment for generating electrical power. Thomas Edison's development of a glowing light bulb and Nikola Tesla's advancements in alternating current (AC) power systems enabled widespread electrification and the creation of the first power grids. These advancements not only illuminated homes but also powered new technologies like Samuel Morse's telegraph, revolutionizing communication. The industrial machinery of the time began relying on electric motors, spurring increased productivity and further embedding electricity as a cornerstone of societal transformation.

As we move into the modern era, electricity has evolved to a driving force behind technological innovation and societal progress. The 20th century witnessed the advent of widespread electrification, enabling advancements such as computing, telecommunications, and household appliances that transformed everyday life. Today, electricity is at the heart of emerging technologies like renewable energy systems, electric vehicles, and smart grids, which aim to address global challenges such as climate change and energy equity. The transition to cleaner, more efficient energy sources underscores the continued importance of electricity as both a fundamental force and a catalyst for progress, shaping a future increasingly defined by connectivity and sustainability.

Let's pause here for a moment and examine the "sustainability" aspect of electricity, particularly how it is produced today. Despite its clean and versatile applications, the origins of electricity reveal a complex relationship with environmental impact. How electricity is generated plays a significant role in determining its sustainability, and this varies widely across the globe.

Currently, most electricity is still derived from fossil fuels like coal, natural gas, and oil. These methods involve burning these fuels to produce heat that drives turbines, creating electricity. While effective at meeting large-scale demand, this process is a major contributor to greenhouse gas emissions, particularly carbon dioxide, exacerbating climate change. Additionally, the extraction and transportation of fossil fuels often lead to severe ecological disruptions, from habitat destruction to oil spills and air pollution, raising questions about the long-term viability of this energy pathway.

Next to that, nuclear power still presents a complex case in the sustainability discussion. It generates electricity with minimal greenhouse gas emissions, making it a potential tool for reducing carbon footprints and providing reliable base-load power. However, its drawbacks are huge, including risks associated with accidents, long-lived radioactive waste, and the environmental costs of uranium extraction and processing. While technological advancements and robust safety measures have mitigated some concerns, questions around waste management and public acceptance remain unresolved.

On the brighter side, renewable energy sources are gaining prominence, with solar, wind, and hydropower leading the charge toward sustainability. These technologies harness natural forces—sunlight, wind, and water flow—to generate electricity without direct emissions of greenhouse gases. Solar panels and wind turbines, for example, produce clean energy during operation, though their production and end-of-life disposal do raise environmental concerns. Renewables are also reshaping the electricity grid, enabling decentralized energy production and increasing energy access in remote areas. As nations set ambitious renewable energy targets, the transition to a cleaner grid seems inevitable, though significant investments in technology and infrastructure remain critical to achieving this goal sustainably.

The rise of electric vehicles (EVs) has been one of the most notable trends in the automotive sector over the past decade. Companies like Tesla have accelerated the shift from traditional internal combustion engine vehicles to electric power, gaining significant market share with their innovative designs and cutting-edge battery technology. As EVs gained traction, governments worldwide have rapidly aligned their policies to support the transition. Many have introduced subsidies and incentives to encourage the adoption of EVs while also pushing for stricter emissions standards. The aim seems to be clear: reduce dependence on oil and fossil fuels, mitigate climate change, and create more sustainable transportation options. However, the push for electric cars is not just about environmental concerns; it is also about controlling energy systems, with electricity grids at the center of this transition.

While governments and industries alike advocate for the widespread adoption of electric cars, they are also strengthening their grip on the electricity infrastructure. EVs rely heavily on the grid for charging, and as more people adopt these vehicles, the demand for electricity is expected to grow exponentially. This is both a challenge and an opportunity for companies and governments to manage and expand the grid's capacity. In some countries, there are concerns that this shift could lead to greater dependence on a centralized grid, potentially turning what was once a vehicle fuel market dominated by oil into a new type of energy dependency. The transition to electric vehicles has spurred investments in charging infrastructure to ensure that EV owners can power their cars efficiently. Some countries have already installed thousands of public charging stations, with more being planned to make the switch to EVs seamless for consumers. This infrastructure expansion, alongside technological advancements in fast-charging and battery efficiency, is helping drive the swift adoption of EVs, but also raises questions about the long-term sustainability of our electricity systems and the true cost of the transition.

Moreover, if you're an electric car owner, take a moment to consider a few key questions. First of all, how many kilometers does your car drive on a single full charge? Most modern electric vehicles today can achieve a range of around 350 to 500 kilometers on a full charge, depending on the specific battery configuration and driving conditions, but other EVs have a more modest range, typically around 250 to 350 kilometers per charge. And do you actually know what a full charge costs you? The cost of charging an EV can vary significantly based on factors like electricity rates in your area, the size of your car's battery, and whether you charge at home or at a public station. It's worth understanding these variables, as they play a crucial role in the overall cost of owning an electric vehicle.

Let's not forget about electric car batteries. While they are designed to last for many years, their performance can degrade over time, potentially resulting in shorter driving ranges and reduced efficiency. Disposal and recycling of these batteries present further challenges, as they contain hazardous materials that require specialized handling. On the positive side, advancements are being made in battery recycling technologies, and companies are exploring ways to reuse materials from old batteries in new ones, reducing the environmental impact of production.

In summary, as EV adoption continues to grow, improvements in battery technology and the development of alternative battery types— such as solid-state batteries—are crucial to making electric cars more sustainable. A more sustainable future for EVs will depend not only on improving the environmental footprint of battery production but also on ensuring that the energy used to power these vehicles comes from renewable sources.

Even bigger problems await the electric flying vehicle industry. They are already facing numerous setbacks, with companies like Lilium and Volocopter encountering significant survival struggles. Lilium, once seen as a leading player in the electric vertical take-off and landing (EVTOL) space, has faced major delays and challenges in achieving its vision. Initially heralded for its sleek design and ambitious goals, Lilium's prototype has struggled to meet safety and regulatory standards, and the company has faced difficulties in scaling its operations. Volocopter, another notable contender, has also encountered its own hurdles, including the complexities of navigating stringent airworthiness certifications, as well as challenges with the scalability of its technology. Both companies have seen their timelines pushed back as they work to address these technical and regulatory obstacles, which has led to skepticism about the feasibility of EVTOLs becoming a mainstream mode of transportation anytime soon.

The rush to develop electric flying vehicles is perhaps, in part, driven by the fear of missing out on the next major breakthrough akin to Tesla's meteoric rise. Entrepreneurs and investors are eager to replicate the success seen in the electric car market, where companies like Tesla have not only disrupted an entire industry but have also reaped substantial financial rewards. However, the complexity and risk involved in these ventures are often overlooked in the race to capitalize on the next big thing.

How about hydrogen-fueled cars as an alternative to EVs? Unlike EVs, which rely on large batteries that require significant mining of rare earth materials, hydrogen fuel cells commonly generate electricity by combining hydrogen and oxygen, emitting only water as a byproduct.

This technology has the potential to complement the existing energy mix, particularly in sectors where electrification faces challenges, such as heavy-duty trucking, aviation, and shipping. However, hydrogen cars face significant hurdles that have slowed their adoption. Producing hydrogen at scale remains energy-intensive, and the current methods still rely on fossil fuels and emit carbon unless combined with carbon capture technologies. "Green hydrogen", produced through water electrolysis powered by renewable energy, offers a cleaner alternative but is still costly and not widely available. Additionally, the infrastructure for hydrogen refueling is sparse compared to the growing network of EV chargers, limiting the practicality of hydrogen cars for most consumers. Hydrogen is also more difficult to store and transport because of the small size of the molecule. So while hydrogen vehicles do hold some promise, their future depends on overcoming the existing challenges and fostering collaboration between industries and governments to improve the production methods and build the necessary infrastructure.

As humanoid robots become increasingly prominent across industries— ranging from manufacturing and logistics to household tasks and personal care—it's worth asking: how are they powered? Companies like Tesla, Boston Dynamics, and Agility Robotics are leading the charge, with innovations that combine advanced AI, robotics, and power systems to enable these robots to operate efficiently.

Powering humanoid robots is a complex challenge that requires balancing energy efficiency, portability, and functionality. Most robots today rely on advanced lithium-ion battery systems, favored for their high energy density and rechargeability. These batteries power motors, sensors, and onboard computing systems, enabling the robots to perform a wide range of tasks. However, the demand for lightweight and durable energy solutions has pushed research toward even more advanced battery chemistries, such as solid-state batteries, which promise improved energy storage and safety.

Beyond batteries, researchers and developers are exploring alternative power sources to overcome the limitations of traditional systems. Hydrogen fuel cells, for example, have emerged as a potential solution for robots that require long operating hours, as they offer high energy output and minimal downtime for refueling. Ever wonder what kind of energy source the Nexus-6 replicants, with a lifespan of four-years, might have relied on?

Another area of focus is energy efficiency. Roboticists are developing lightweight materials and more efficient actuators to reduce power consumption. The components responsible for movement are a primary energy drain, so improving their design and control systems has a direct impact on battery life. AI-driven energy management systems are also being integrated to optimize power usage in real-time, ensuring that robots can prioritize essential tasks and conserve energy when idle.

All in all, as humanoid robots become more versatile and integrated into daily life, advancements in power systems will be crucial to overcoming current limitations. But how long will it truly take for fully functional humanoids to become part of our everyday reality? While some entrepreneurs suggest rapid progress, it's wise to remain cautious— there's still a long way to go before these technologies become practical, affordable, and widely accepted. That said, the future possibilities are undeniably intriguing. Could humanoid robots enrich our lives or introduce unforeseen challenges? How do you feel about their growing presence and potential role in our world? And do you think a world like Westworld, where humanoid robots seamlessly blend with humans, can ever become a reality?

As we move forward with the rapid development of electric cars, humanoid robots, and other emerging technologies, it's vital to consider one essential question: will we continue down the path of producing cheap, disposable products that break down quickly, forcing consumers to buy more, or will we move toward creating durable goods designed to last longer? The impact of such decisions stretches far beyond the immediate convenience of lower costs. From the batteries in electric vehicles to the materials used in robots, the environmental cost of shorter product lifespans and wasteful consumption is something we must face head-on. It's a challenge that requires a shift in how we think about product design, energy use, and sustainability. And as you consider your own role in this transformation, think about the items you purchase—whether it's your car, your clothes, or the technology in your home. How long do you expect your purchases to last, and what happens when they're no longer useful?

In general, we should strive to consume less and place greater value on the quality, longevity, and purposeful use of the items we purchase. Prioritizing thoughtful consumption over constant acquisition can help foster a culture of responsibility and reduce unnecessary waste. You can do this!

III

Utopia

15

The Good

Imagine a world where everyone is born into equal opportunities. Regardless of where someone lives or their family's circumstances, every child has access to excellent education and healthcare. The divisions of race, gender, and class no longer dictate a person's potential. Societies have dismantled the systems that once perpetuated discrimination, replacing them with structures that promote fairness and shared humanity. People celebrate diversity, recognizing that differences enrich the collective experience rather than divide it. Progress is measured not by individual achievements but by how inclusive and supportive communities have become. In this world, collaboration replaces competition as the cornerstone of success.

Physical borders no longer define where one can go or what one can achieve. Nations still celebrate their unique cultures and histories, but humanity now operates as a single, interconnected entity. Migration is no longer feared; it is embraced as an exchange of ideas, skills, and traditions. Refugees and migrants are welcomed with open arms, supported as they build new lives that contribute to the communities they join. Airports and train stations are places of opportunity, not checkpoints of suspicion. The concept of belonging shifts from geography to shared goals and values. This global openness fosters a sense of unity that humanity has never known before.

With equality and shared purpose at the forefront, violence becomes a relic of the past. Conflict is resolved through open dialogue, facilitated by neutral mediators trained in conflict resolution and restorative justice. Global disarmament treaties are not just signed but upheld, leading to the dismantling of the arms trade. The resources once spent on war are redirected toward education, healthcare, and environmental restoration. Communities thrive on mutual trust, supported by robust mental health initiatives that address the roots of interpersonal violence. Streets are safe, homes are harmonious, and peace becomes the new normal.

Governance transforms into a service tailored to its citizens. Imagine a world where policies are not dictated by backroom deals but crafted through real-time public participation. Advanced technologies allow citizens to vote on local and global issues with ease, ensuring their voices are heard. Technology guarantees transparency in government spending, eradicating corruption. Leaders are chosen for their wisdom, empathy, and vision, and the archaic influence of wealth and connections on politics fades into history. People feel empowered, knowing that their governments serve them and uphold the principles of fairness, justice, and progress.

Money as we know it becomes obsolete. With automation driving production costs to near zero, essential goods and services like food, housing, and healthcare are universally accessible. Instead of chasing paychecks, people pursue their passions, dedicating time to art, science, and community-building. Cooperation becomes the new currency, as societies measure wealth not by material possessions but by the collective well-being of their citizens. Stress over financial survival disappears, replaced by a sense of security and fulfillment.

Nature, once on the brink of collapse, is revitalized. Renewable energy powers the world, eliminating the need for fossil fuels. Cities are transformed into green havens, with vertical gardens and urban forests cleaning the air and enriching daily life. Wildlife corridors reconnect ecosystems, allowing species to thrive again. Oceans, once overfished and polluted, teem with life. Humanity learns to coexist with nature, not as a dominator but as a steward, preserving its beauty and resources for future generations. A balance is struck, creating a world where the environment and civilization flourish together.

In this future, privacy is a right protected by technology. Data is no longer commodified or stolen but used responsibly with explicit consent. Encrypted communication allows individuals to express themselves freely without fear of surveillance. Governments operate transparently, earning the trust of their citizens. Creativity flourishes in this environment, as people feel safe to share their ideas and challenge norms. Personal freedom and collective transparency coexist harmoniously, creating a digital landscape built on respect and accountability.

Technology becomes an equalizer, breaking down barriers that once divided people. Digital platforms bring education and healthcare to even the most remote corners of the world. A child in a rural village can learn from the same world-class instructors as a student in a metropolitan city, while AI-powered doctors provide personalized care to patients anywhere. The digital divide becomes a relic of the past, as universal access to technology empowers everyone to connect, collaborate, and innovate. This interconnectedness fosters global problem-solving and a sense of shared responsibility.

Wealth no longer pools in the hands of a few but is distributed in ways that ensure everyone has what they need to thrive. Universal basic income provides security, while progressive solutions fund public goods like education, healthcare, and infrastructure. Philanthropy shifts from acts of charity to systemic change, addressing the roots of inequality. People feel valued not for what they own but for how they contribute to their communities. Economic systems prioritize collective success, and societies measure progress by well-being rather than GDP.

Governments operate with the efficiency of a well-run organization, delivering services seamlessly to their citizens. Imagine a world where renewing a passport, starting a business, or accessing social benefits takes just minutes. AI and data-driven insights optimize public services, ensuring resources reach those who need them most. Citizens are no longer passive recipients of governance but active participants, shaping policies that reflect their needs and values. This participatory approach restores trust and fosters a sense of shared ownership over society's direction.

Automation frees humanity from the drudgery of repetitive and dangerous work. Robots handle mundane tasks, allowing people to focus on creativity, relationships, and innovation. A basic income ensures that no one is left behind in this transition. Work becomes a choice, driven by passion and purpose rather than necessity. Industries reorient themselves to prioritize human well-being, and society thrives as people discover new ways to contribute meaningfully without the constraints of survival-based labor.

Food production undergoes a revolution. Hunger and malnutrition are eradicated, while biodiversity is restored as industrial farming practices give way to eco-friendly innovations. Urban centers feature vertical farms that provide fresh produce locally, reducing waste and emissions. Modern solutions ensure that everyone has access to nutritious, sustainable food, and eating becomes an act of uniting communities in a shared appreciation for health and sustainability.

Global crises no longer spiral out of control. Humanity unites to tackle challenges like climate change and pandemics, guided by a shared sense of responsibility. International collaboration leads to breakthroughs in renewable energy, healthcare, and disaster response. Scientists, leaders, and citizens work hand in hand, driven by hope. The world becomes a place where crises are met with resilience and solidarity, demonstrating the strength of collective action.

Artificial intelligence and humanity form a harmonious partnership. Machines augment human creativity, solving problems and enhancing daily life. AI-powered tools help design new medicines and tackle societal challenges. Ethical frameworks ensure that technology serves people rather than exploiting them. In this future, humans are not replaced by machines but elevated by them, creating a society that blends innovation with compassion and progress with purpose.

16

The Bad

Equality remains an elusive goal. Despite some progress, systemic barriers persist, keeping vast segments of the population trapped in cycles of poverty and discrimination. Wealthier nations boast advancements in education and healthcare, but these remain inaccessible luxuries for many in poorer regions. Social hierarchies based on race, gender, and class subtly yet firmly dictate opportunities. Public debates about equality are loud and divisive, often resulting in symbolic gestures rather than meaningful change. While some individuals break through systemic barriers, the majority still struggle under the weight of entrenched inequality.

Borders harden as nationalism and economic self-interest dominate global politics. Migration policies grow increasingly restrictive, fueled by fear and political rhetoric rather than compassion or logic. Refugees fleeing war, climate disasters, and persecution find themselves stranded in overcrowded camps or turned away entirely. Nations build walls—physical and metaphorical—claiming to protect their sovereignty but deepening divisions in the process. Travel becomes less about cultural exchange and more about navigating bureaucratic hurdles, with passports and visas reinforcing a growing sense of "us versus them".

Violence remains an inescapable part of daily life for many. Local conflicts simmer as governments struggle to address the root causes of unrest. Systemic violence persists in the form of police brutality, discriminatory laws, and unchecked corporate exploitation. The global arms trade continues unabated, arming militias and authoritarian regimes alike. While outright war between major nations is rare, proxy conflicts and regional skirmishes keep millions in fear. In communities, interpersonal violence is fueled by rising inequality and untreated mental health issues, leaving even the most developed societies unable to feel truly safe.

Governance becomes a theater of inefficiency and stagnation. Politicians make grand promises but deliver little, as corruption and bureaucracy suppress meaningful reform. Technology is introduced into governance, but it is poorly implemented, often worsening existing inefficiencies rather than solving them. Citizens feel increasingly alienated from decision-making processes, watching as policies benefit corporations and elites rather than the public. Trust in democracy erodes, with voter turnout declining and apathy spreading as people lose faith in their governments' ability to enact meaningful change.

Money continues to rule people's lives, perpetuating stress and inequity. Economic growth slows, and the wealth gap widens as the rich find new ways to consolidate their power. The majority work longer hours for stagnant wages, unable to afford rising costs for essentials like housing and healthcare. Financial systems remain fragile, prone to crashes that disproportionately harm the most vulnerable. Debt becomes a near-universal experience, chaining individuals and families to a system that feels impossible to escape. Dreams of financial stability remain out of reach for many, breeding resentment and hopelessness.

Nature suffers from neglect and half-hearted solutions. Climate agreements are signed but poorly enforced, leaving emissions to rise and ecosystems to falter. Biodiversity continues to decline, with species disappearing at an alarming rate. Natural disasters, from hurricanes to wildfires, grow more frequent and devastating, hitting the poorest communities hardest. While renewable energy makes progress, it is not adopted quickly enough to halt environmental degradation. Greenwashing becomes commonplace, as corporations mask their destructive practices with superficial eco-friendly initiatives.

Privacy becomes a luxury rather than a right. Surveillance capitalism thrives as governments and corporations expand their ability to collect, analyze, and profit from personal data. While some laws are passed to curb the worst abuses, loopholes abound, leaving individuals vulnerable to digital exploitation. Anonymity becomes harder to maintain, and self-censorship rises as people fear the consequences of their online actions. The digital world feels less like a space of freedom and more like a monitored platform where every click is tracked and monetized.

Technology deepens divides rather than bridging them. Wealthier countries and privileged communities enjoy the benefits of advanced tools, while poorer regions remain disconnected or reliant on outdated systems. Education and healthcare are increasingly digitized, but access remains uneven, leaving millions excluded. The promise of universal connectivity feels hollow as the digital divide persists, reinforcing existing inequalities. Those with access to cutting-edge technologies pull further ahead, creating a world where opportunity depends not just on talent but on internet speed and device quality.

Wealth continues to concentrate in the hands of the few. Efforts to implement redistributive policies like universal basic income or progressive taxation meet fierce resistance from entrenched interests. Philanthropy, while helpful in isolated cases, fails to address structural issues, often serving as a public relations tool for the ultra-wealthy. Economic mobility grinds to a halt, with class divides becoming more rigid. For the majority, life feels like an uphill battle, while the elite live in a bubble of privilege, disconnected from the struggles of the rest of humanity.

Governments adopt technology to streamline services but fail to implement it effectively. Bureaucratic inefficiencies persist, with AI systems often biased or poorly maintained, leading to inequitable outcomes. Citizens grow frustrated as promises of smart governance fall short, and traditional systems remain slow and unresponsive. Access to essential services like healthcare or benefits becomes more difficult for those without digital literacy, leaving vulnerable populations further marginalized. Trust in governance continues to erode, as technological solutions feel like empty gestures rather than meaningful reforms.

Automation disrupts industries but leaves millions behind. Jobs in manufacturing, retail, and even professional sectors are replaced by machines, with little support for displaced workers. Social safety nets struggle to keep pace, and many are left scrambling for employment in an increasingly automated world. Those who find work often do so in precarious gig economy jobs, with low pay and no benefits. Society grows increasingly polarized between those who benefit from automation and those who are left behind, creating a sense of instability and discontent.

Food systems strain under the weight of rising populations and environmental pressures. Industrial farming continues to dominate, leading to soil depletion, water scarcity, and biodiversity loss. While technological advancements promise solutions, they are slow to be adopted or remain accessible only to wealthy nations. Malnutrition persists in poorer regions, while wealthier areas face health crises linked to over-processed foods. The global food supply chain remains vulnerable to shocks, causing periodic shortages and price spikes that disproportionately harm the most vulnerable.

Crises like pandemics and climate disasters are met with fragmented, reactionary responses. Nations prioritize their own interests, undermining global collaboration. Healthcare systems buckle under pressure, and vaccine distribution favors wealthier countries, leaving others to fend for themselves. Climate mitigation efforts are slow and insufficient, with nations bickering over responsibilities and resources. As crises grow more frequent, humanity appears caught in a cycle of response rather than prevention, unable to build the resilience needed for the challenges ahead.

Artificial intelligence advances but deepens existing inequalities. High-tech tools are primarily developed and controlled by corporations, prioritizing profit over public benefit. AI systems are used to automate surveillance, manipulate markets, and influence public opinion, often with harmful consequences. Job displacement accelerates, with few safeguards in place to support those affected. Biases embedded in algorithms perpetuate discrimination, making life harder for marginalized communities. While AI has the potential to revolutionize society, its benefits remain unevenly distributed, aggravating divisions rather than bridging them.

17

The Ugly

Equality becomes a distant dream as humanity fractures into rigid hierarchies. Wealth, race, and status determine every aspect of a person's life, from the opportunities they can access to the respect they are afforded. The privileged elite live in fortified enclaves, enjoying unimaginable luxuries, while the vast majority struggle in sprawling slums or desolate rural areas. Discrimination is not just tolerated but institutionalized, as systems of power are designed to perpetuate the divide. In this world, being born into the wrong circumstances is a life sentence, with no hope of escape.

Borders become battle lines, fiercely defended with military force and cutting-edge technology. Refugees and migrants are met with violence as they try to flee unlivable conditions. Desperate people are trapped in vast, overcrowded camps, forgotten by the world. Smugglers and human traffickers thrive as the only means of escape, creating a new shadow economy of exploitation. Nations isolate themselves entirely, cutting off communication and trade, fostering hostility and paranoia. International collaboration becomes a thing of the past as countries focus solely on their own survival.

Violence is omnipresent. Wars rage across the globe as nations, corporations, and rogue factions fight over dwindling resources. Autonomous weapons wreak havoc on civilian populations, and entire regions are reduced to wastelands. Crime flourishes in cities where law enforcement has collapsed or become brutally authoritarian. Personal safety becomes a luxury, with even small acts of daily life fraught with danger. People live in constant fear, not just of war but of their neighbors, as trust erodes and survival instincts take over.

Governance collapses into authoritarian regimes or outright anarchy. In some places, despots rule with an iron fist, suppressing dissent with mass surveillance and violent crackdowns. In others, governments cease to function entirely, leaving power vacuums filled by warlords, cartels, or corporations. Corruption is rampant, with public officials serving only themselves and their allies. Citizens have no voice, no recourse, and no hope for change. Governance no longer exists to serve the people—it exists solely to maintain control over them.

Money becomes a weapon of oppression. The global economy collapses into hyper-capitalism, where the rich control every resource and the poor are left to fend for scraps. Basic needs like food, water, and shelter are commodified to the point where only the wealthiest can afford them. Debt is used as a tool to enslave entire populations, forcing people into labor camps or perpetual servitude. Financial systems are rigged to ensure that the elite grow ever richer while the masses grow ever poorer.

Nature is ravaged beyond repair. Climate change accelerates unchecked, leading to catastrophic weather events that devastate entire regions. Forests are burned to the ground for short-term profits, oceans are choked with plastic and devoid of life, and arable land becomes scarce. Mass extinctions wipe out countless species, including those critical to ecosystems humans depend on. Resource scarcity leads to brutal wars, and billions are displaced by floods, droughts, and unlivable temperatures.

Privacy is completely eradicated in the name of security and control. Governments and corporations monitor every aspect of daily life, using AI to predict and suppress dissent. Dissenters are identified and silenced before they can organize, creating a climate of fear and conformity. Personal data is sold to the highest bidder, fueling a predatory economy that exploits individuals at every turn. Anonymity becomes impossible, and self-censorship pervades every interaction. The digital world is no longer a tool for connection but a panopticon of oppression.

Technology deteriorates inequality, with the rich living in futuristic utopias while the poor are trapped in a dystopian nightmare. Advanced healthcare and education are available only to those who can pay, leaving the rest of humanity to suffer from preventable diseases and ignorance. AI-controlled systems prioritize profits over people, automating exploitation and eliminating jobs. Entire populations are left with no access to technology, widening the gap between the haves and have-nots. Innovation becomes a privilege, and the digital divide becomes an uncrossable chasm.

Wealth becomes a tool of domination. The elite use their resources to control politics, media, and industry, shaping the world to serve their interests. The poor are stripped of their rights and reduced to mere laborers or consumers in a system designed to exploit them. Efforts to redistribute wealth are met with violent resistance, and philanthropy becomes a façade for maintaining power. The majority of humanity lives in desperate poverty, while the elite grow increasingly detached from reality in their fortified mansions and private paradises.

Governments devolve into bureaucratic nightmares or tools of oppression. Services are inaccessible to most citizens, and those that do exist are riddled with inefficiency and corruption. AI-powered systems prioritize surveillance and control over providing meaningful services. Vulnerable populations are excluded entirely, left to navigate a chaotic and hostile world on their own. Trust in governance is nonexistent, and society fractures into isolated, self-interested groups, each fending for itself.

Automation creates a new form of slavery. Robots and AI replace workers in every sector, but instead of liberating humanity, they entrench inequality. The elite benefit from increased productivity, while the majority are left unemployed and destitute. Gig economy jobs become the only option for survival, offering meager pay and no security. Entire industries collapse, leaving communities abandoned and economies in ruins. Automation becomes a tool of oppression, concentrating wealth and power in the hands of a few.

Food systems collapse, leading to widespread famine and malnutrition. Industrial farming devastates ecosystems, leaving the land unable to support life. Climate change disrupts global supply chains, causing shortages and skyrocketing prices. Wealthy nations hoard what little food remains, while billions go hungry. Genetically modified crops become the only viable option, controlled by corporations that exploit their monopoly. Eating becomes an act of desperation rather than nourishment, as people scramble to find enough to survive.

Global crises spiral out of control. Pandemics sweep through unprepared healthcare systems, leaving countless dead. Climate disasters displace entire populations, creating waves of refugees that no nation is willing to accept. Resource wars break out as nations and corporations fight over dwindling supplies of water, oil, and minerals. Humanity fails to unite against these challenges, instead fracturing into warring factions. Crises become the new normal, and the world descends into chaos.

Artificial intelligence becomes humanity's master rather than its servant. Autonomous systems enforce authoritarian rule, monitoring every move and eliminating dissent. AI-powered weapons decimate communities, targeting entire regions with precision. Machines replace humans in decision-making, prioritizing efficiency over empathy. Humanity becomes subservient to technology, with no control over the systems that govern their lives. In this world, the promise of AI as a tool for progress is twisted into a nightmare of domination and despair.

18

What Now?

What kind of world do you want to live in?

A world where equality, cooperation, and progress lead to a brighter future—or one where division, greed, and apathy leave us spiraling into chaos? The future isn't written in stone; it's shaped by the choices we make today. Every action, no matter how small, contributes to the trajectory of our societies. Will you choose to be a bystander, allowing the forces of inertia to dictate the course of history? Or will you actively participate in creating a world that reflects the values you hold dear?

This is not a question for governments or corporations alone—it is a question for each of us. The decisions we make in our daily lives, from how we engage with our communities to the causes we support, ripple outward in ways we cannot always see. The good, the bad, and the ugly scenarios presented are not inevitable outcomes. They are possibilities, warnings, and calls to action. It is within your power, as an individual and as part of a collective, to steer the world toward a future worth living in.

If we ever hope to realize the good scenario—a world of equality, sustainability, and shared prosperity—radical action is not just desirable, it is essential. This does not mean violence or destruction, but a peaceful yet relentless uprising of humanity's collective will. Millions, perhaps billions, of people must come together to challenge the systems that perpetuate inequality, environmental degradation, and unchecked power. The absurdities of our current world—where profit outweighs human dignity, where resources are hoarded by the few, and where nature is treated as disposable—cannot be solved through incremental change alone. Now is the time to rise above complacency and act with conviction, determination, and unity.

Opposing what is wrong is just the first step. Protests, petitions, and movements that call out injustice are vital, but they must be matched by an equally powerful drive to build alternatives. It is not enough to say "no" to the systems that harm us; we must also create and scale solutions that reflect the world we want to live in. Imagine millions of people mobilizing not just to block harmful policies but to establish new systems of governance, economics, and technology that prioritize people and planet over profit. The change must be thorough and profound—addressing the root causes of our crises rather than merely treating their symptoms.

This requires courage and collaboration on an unprecedented scale. It means bridging divides, breaking down silos, and refusing to be distracted by the forces that seek to divide us. The challenges we face—climate collapse, growing inequality, and the erosion of freedoms—are vast, but so is the power of humanity when it works together. The time to act is now, not tomorrow or the next election cycle. Change begins with each of us, but it gains unstoppable momentum when we join forces. Together, we can dismantle what is broken and build something extraordinary in its place.

We, the people, outnumber the elite few who seek to control the world for their own gain. They may possess vast wealth and wield immense influence, but their power is built on the illusion that the majority will remain passive. What they lack—and what we possess in abundance—is the strength of numbers, fueled by our shared energy, love, passion, and intellect. These are forces that no amount of money or manipulation can suppress. When billions of voices, hearts, and minds unite, they form a movement that cannot be ignored, outmaneuvered, or outcompeted.

The future belongs to those who believe in it enough to fight for it. By combining our creativity, determination, and unwavering hope, we have the potential to reshape the world in ways that serve everyone, not just the privileged few. Our collective power lies not only in resistance but in creation—building a future where cooperation replaces exploitation, and where the well-being of the many outweighs the greed of the few. This is a call to awaken to our strength, to recognize that together, we are a force more powerful than any system designed to divide us. When the majority rises with unity and purpose, no elite, however wealthy or powerful, can stand in the way of real and lasting change.

Yes, we all have our differences—our backgrounds, beliefs, cultures, and perspectives. But these differences are not weaknesses; they are strengths. They are the threads that weave the rich tapestry of humanity, offering diverse ideas, solutions, and experiences. It is natural to disagree on certain things, and that's not a problem. Disagreement, when handled with respect and empathy, is not a barrier but a bridge—a way to learn from one another and grow together. What matters most is that we uphold the dignity and freedom of each person, recognizing that no one has a monopoly on truth and everyone deserves the liberty to live their life freely.

But despite our differences, we can unite. There is more that binds us together than separates us: our shared humanity, our desire for safety and opportunity, and our hope for a better future for ourselves and those who come after us. When we focus on these commonalities, we discover that we are far more powerful as a collective than as individuals. Unity doesn't mean uniformity—it means embracing our diversity while working toward shared goals. By standing together with respect and compassion, we can build a future that honors everyone's uniqueness while ensuring that no one is left behind.

The question of how to unite remains one of the most difficult challenges we face. If the answer were clear, we might already be well on our way to building the future we long for. But the enormity of the task—the sheer scale of the systems we need to change and the forces we must overcome—can feel paralyzing. It's easy to believe that making a difference is impossible, that the efforts of a single individual or even a small group of dedicated activists are insignificant in the face of such overwhelming odds. This sense of powerlessness is precisely what allows the status quo to persist, as millions of people, disheartened and doubtful, hesitate to act.

But the truth is, we cannot afford to let fear or doubt hold us back. This is not the time for small steps or isolated efforts; it is the time for something extraordinary. We need to take our union to a level that defies expectations—a level that combines our voices, talents, and resources into a force so powerful it cannot be ignored. Imagine millions, even billions, of people mobilizing, not in scattered protests but in coordinated action that transcends borders, ideologies, and divisions. This kind of unity, born of urgency and purpose, is what will break through the barriers that now seem insurmountable. It is not just about opposing what is wrong but about creating something new—together.

Critics might dismiss these ideas as "wishful thinking," "utopian," or even "populistic." And sure, from a certain perspective, they do seem unrealistic—a grand vision too ambitious to materialize. But what if this is the only way to truly change things? What if embracing this kind of collective action, however improbable it may appear, is humanity's best chance to rewrite its future? To reject it outright as impossible is to miss out on the greatest opportunity we might ever have to build a better world. The road ahead is undoubtedly difficult, but isn't the risk of failure preferable to the certainty of remaining trapped in systems that harm us all? Change begins with imagination, and from imagination comes action—and from action, transformation. This is no time to let doubt win; it is a time to dare.

Perhaps the first step for all of us is simply to let these ideas sink in. Reflect on them, question them, laugh at their idealism, or even ridicule them if you must. That's okay—skepticism is part of the process. But after the initial reaction, perhaps a small voice in the back of your mind will begin to whisper: What if this isn't so wrong? What if there's something here worth considering? Because when you take a step back and look at the world as it is, what are the alternatives? Do you sincerely believe that we're on a path of global progress and positivity?

This book is written with the intention of remaining hopeful and optimistic, because hope is essential. But let's be honest with ourselves—hope alone may not be enough. The challenges we face are enormous, and the systems in place are deeply entrenched. Miracles seem in short supply, and we need more than one to get to a better place. Yet, miracles begin with people daring to dream and act in ways that others once thought impossible. So maybe, just maybe, the miracle we need starts with us—each of us—inching closer to a shared vision of something better, something worth fighting for.

In a world increasingly dominated by division and disconnection, one of the simplest acts we can undertake is to find each other. Building meaningful connections across distances and differences has the potential to spark collective action and inspire change. By using the hashtag **#TakeMeToNaboo**, we can start leaving behind breadcrumbs and create a shared thread—a way for like-minded individuals to identify, interact, and grow together. Whether it's put on a T-shirt, shared in a post, or mentioned in a conversation, the hashtag can act as a beacon, signaling to others who yearn for something more— hope, action, and connection. It offers a starting point for dialogue, collaboration, and community-building. So use the hashtag wherever it feels right, and let it help bridge the gaps as we move closer to a shared vision of hope, connection, and action.

Looking forward to finding you out there!

About the Author

Drake Tandrist is a modern Renaissance man whose diverse passions span arts, literature, science, and humanism. A middle-aged visionary with a boundless curiosity for the world, he is known for his unstoppable optimism and unwavering belief in humanity's potential to create a better future.

Drake's deep commitment to justice and his passion for innovation drive his work as a thinker, creator, and changemaker. With a talent for thinking outside the box, he has developed a reputation for challenging conventions and inspiring people to see possibilities where others see limitations.

Through the smart and thoughtful application of technology, Drake consistently seeks to design solutions that empower individuals and communities, always with an eye toward driving positive, lasting change. Whether crafting new ideas, building systems that bridge disciplines, or encouraging others to embrace bold thinking, his creative spirit is at the heart of everything he does.

Drake's life philosophy reflects his enduring belief in the power of human creativity and resilience to overcome challenges and shape a brighter future. Take Me to Naboo is a testament to his vision and a call to action for all who dream of a more compassionate, equitable, and innovative world.